GAUDI

© *1984 Ediciones Polígrafa, S. A.*

Balmes, 54 - Barcelona-7 (Spain)

Translation by Kenneth Lyons

I.S.B.N.: 84-343-0388-4
Dep. Leg.: B. 33.680 - 1986 (Printed in Spain)

Printed in Spain by La Polígrafa, S. A. - Parets del Vallès (Barcelona)

Ignasi de Solà-Morales

GAUDI

Photographs: F. Català-Roca

EDICIONES POLIGRAFA, S. A.

Publisher's Note

We wish to express our thanks to the Gaudí Chair of the Higher Technical School of Architecture of Barcelona and to its present incumbent, Don Juan Bassegoda Nonell, for the cooperation given in obtaining the graphic and documentary material for this book.

View of Barcelona.

An architecture for a city

The architectural work of Gaudí is inseparable from the city of Barcelona. Although not all of his great works were built in this city, it is certainly a fact that his total *œuvre* cannot be understood unless we establish a direct relationship with all the aspirations and transformations that affected the city between the last quarter of the 19th century and the second decade of the 20th.

Architecture is never a phenomenon enclosed in itself but a social manifestation. The form and language of this manifestation are inseparable from the objectives and aspirations that prevail at certain levels of the class, or classes, in power at a given moment in history. But this does not come about by chance, nor yet as the result of a direct connection between the ideas collectively dominating a particular historical period and the physical shape of that period's architectural objects, for any such connection is mediated by the urban surroundings in which the architecture is actually built. Thus the first explicative relationship that we must establish in order to understand the work of Gaudí is undoubtedly that between this work and the city in which it was produced — with an analysis, at the same time, of the circumstances of the city in Gaudí's day and the explanation of these circumstances that we can find in architecture as the plastic language of urban space.

Throughout the 19th century Barcelona was constantly expanding. With the pulling down of the old walls in 1854 and, later, the laying out of the 'Extension Plan' proposed by Ildefons Cerdà, the municipal area grew from less than twenty hectares to a potential of over two hundred. The driving forces behind this expansion were the cotton, iron and steel industries, whose need for workers produced a steady flow of immigration. Between 1850 and 1900 the population quadrupled, rising from 150,000 inhabitants to 600,000, who occupied the historic central area of the city and, at a rapidly increasing rate, the new buildings in the original 'Plain' of Barcelona, now laid out in the grid pattern established in the Extension Plan (El Ensanche).

The industries, moreover, were also moving their factories from their original situation on the outskirts of the walled city to some of the nearby villages, thus creating a rough circle of industrial districts beyond the limits of the Ensanche — the use of which for industry was never more than secondary. In this way districts or villages like Sants, Sant Andreu, Gràcia and the Barceloneta formed the new periphery of an urban structure of a very dynamic kind

5

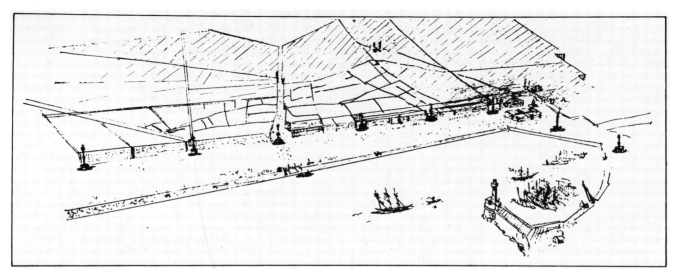

Bird's-eye view of the sea front of Barcelona. Drawing by Gaudí for his project for the illumination of the Sea Wall (1891).

which still had to be formed in each and every one of its elements.

This new city, which the people of 19th-century Barcelona saw growing at such a tremendous rate, had to reappraise its more important services, its monuments and its most representative public buildings in order to conform to the idea of a city that was definitely taking on the characteristics of a great metropolitan centre.

Really, however, the urban development of Barcelona is simply the most concentrated — and therefore the most visible — aspect in the process of the transformation of a whole region. When Pierre Vilar speaks of the transformations in the region of Barcelona, he is also referring to that of all the nearby areas, which were completely drawn into the same process; and the consequence of this process, in the fields of transport, energy and trade, was to be the foundation of a metropolitan area eager to share, as regards both town planning and culture, in the same adventure of modernity.

The transformations involved in Barcelona's development into a metropolis also affected the form of its principal historic districts. The port, the old fortress of the Ciutadella, the very fabric of the historic city, had to adapt to the new metropolitan scale being assumed by the modern town. The process included great changes in the relationship between the city and its port, the laying out of the first large-scale municipal park and the opening of great new streets, their width and straightness ensuring faster traffic, through the old maze of medieval lanes and alleys which had hitherto been enclosed by the city walls. I am making all these references because these were the sites, the spaces old and new, on which Gaudí was to work and in the characterization of which he was to insert his own conception of architecture, his own contribution to the formation of the backdrop, so to speak, against which the new metropolitan life was to be lived. But the new city, too, was to be an architectural problem. Both the districts that grew up in the vast network of the Cerdà Ensanche and the more distant areas that formed the industrial

ring around Barcelona proper, and awaited their turn in the incessant enlargement brought about by the growing population, were to contain examples of Gaudí's architecture. Blocks of flats, detached houses for gentlemen, churches and schools, housing estates for workers and new garden suburbs: these were some of the things the new metropolis needed. And Gaudí, far from eluding the problems they presented, always endeavoured to solve them in the way best suited to the new urban concepts and demands.

The Barcelona of that time, rapidly becoming one of the most important metropolitan areas in the Mediterranean world, was marked by a profoundly-felt optimism. The newly ascendant industrial bourgeoisie had consolidated their power in Catalonia after the restoration of the constitutional monarchy in 1874 and the end of the civil wars in 1876. Catalonia's essential difference from the rest of the Spanish state was at the root of the tensions between Catalan nationalism and desire for autonomy, on the one hand, and the reformism of the state as a whole, on the other. The metropolitan expansion that was the setting for Gaudí's work was in itself a political project. It was an attempt to give shape to the image of a new class, that of the industrial entrepreneurs who, in their newfound social predominance, wanted to endow the city with a form and an architectural image that would reflect their ability to transform the relationships of production, the social structure and the space in which those relationships and that structure existed. The optimism of the members of this new class, with their faith in economic progress and in the capacity of reason to cope with the new situations, showed itself in the efforts made to give material form to their aspirations through a veritable explosion of creative activities. The artists were called upon to provide a tangible fulfilment of those aspirations and to expound the characteristics of the new social order in comprehensible fashion. The role of art and architecture, like those of other cultural activities, was to be quite clearly linked to these ideas. A contribution to the new age, to this new period of wealth and welfare, progress and expansion, was the most profound ideal for which the new ruling class wanted its artists and intellectuals to work.

But this general picture of optimism in the creation of a new social order was not in fact reflected, on the part of the artists, by an equally optimistic and harmonious response showing their unlimited confidence in the future. On the contrary, indeed, both in the architecture of Gaudí and in other manifestations of the restoration period, the forward-looking optimism that characterized the culture of this 19th century industrial bourgeoisie was tempered by a critical conscience that was just as incisive and radical.

The period of Catalan culture during which Gaudí's work was produced, was that of the movement known in Catalonia as *Modernisme*, which was more or less the local name for *Art Nouveau*. As was the case in other great cities of Europe — Paris, Vienna, Brussels, Milan, Glasgow, etc. — the *Modernisme* of Catalonia really represented, both in the field of literature and in that of the plastic arts, a general loss of confidence in 19th century cultural models and an attempt by the artists to express themselves in a language that would be at once genuine and elitist in relation to society as a whole.

Modernisme always had a strong tinge of Catalan nationalism and its roots were supposed to be in a native tradition which some Catalans were now trying to revive. In this seems to lie its first problem: that of its cultural identity. As against the indiscriminate consumption of the universal culture of all ages that was preached by the progressive elements, *Modernisme* endeavoured to express specific characteristics of its own — the sort of manners, traditions or ''spirit of place'' that did not contribute to the universalism of the imperialistic capitalism of the time but, on the contrary, sought to go more deeply into everything local and vernacular, thus expressing these artists' criticism of the uniformity inevitably established by an industrial civilization.

Thus, the problem of tradition in *Modérnisme* — and in Gaudí — sounds the first note of criticism of the industrial bourgeoisie's thrusting optimism. It established a more complex, dialectical relationship

Pablo Picasso: *Charity.* C. 1899. Drawing on paper, 22.9 × 33.5 cm. Picasso Museum, Barcelona.

between tradition and innovation, introducing a mediating element between absolute novelty and change, on the one hand, and sheer reactionary immobilism, on the other.

Another aspect which should not be neglected is that of the *Modernista* view of society. The great new metropolis did not develop as a harmonious whole, but was in fact plagued with contradictions and dysfunctions which can be detected and visualized in the more negative aspects of the industrial world. There was, in the first place, what today we might call the fringe society. Alongside the dazzling new splendour of the great cities — Barcelona among them — there was often dreadful poverty. At this time, indeed, the poor, the fringe dwellers, the frightful slums, dirt and unhygienic conditions, disease and loneliness all went to make up a phenomenon of increasing proportions. The paintings of Nonell, or those of Picasso's Barcelona period, dealt with the life of the fringe society, not gratuitously but as their response to a real and disquieting aspect of the developing metropolitan society. In Gaudí, too, the problems of the misfits and the poor were subjects that were to be expressed more and more in his work through his stylization of the elemental and the way he resorted to poor, coarse materials in his externalization of the anguished compassion that moved the intellectuals of the period. It is true, of course, that at first glance *Modernisme*, like the parallel movements in other European cities, will seem to be almost exclusively an explosion of splendour and luxury, a wealth of decoration, a sumptuous and gratuitous display of ornamentation. Yet both the ornamental motifs in the applied arts and the brilliant, exuberant use of colour in painting did not simply reflect the confident enthusiasm of the new ruling class but also revealed a pure, agonizing insecurity and an explicit fragility.

Any relationship with nature had become difficult and remote, while the dynamism of the urban world was chaotic in its constant change. All security and order seemed to have vanished, giving place to an aggressive, competitive atmosphere, in which no amount of decorative magnificence could conceal the disturbing presence of the uncontrollable, the irrational and the contradictory.

It was surely not by pure chance that the art of the *Modernista* period was so favourably re-examined by the Surrealists, who saw in it an early expression of their own dissatisfaction, their own critical stance regarding the gay, cocksure culture of the bourgeoisie.

In the case of Gaudí this critical and insecure attitude crystallized, as his work became more mature, into the religious and social Utopianism of a Catholic faith that was militantly reformist in its attitude to contemporary metropolitan life. He gradually came to be more and more closely associated with the circle of thinkers and social reformers who, inspired by a renewed Catholic doctrine, tenaciously endeavoured, from within the system itself, to put a moderately critical curb on the optimism of 19th-century progressivism. Since he was inclined to be pessimistic about the human condition, and came to reveal increasingly redemptorist intentions in his art, in the context of *Modernista* culture Gaudí's work exemplified an attitude that was in fact both critical and significant in respect of the more properly aestheticist positions typical of the European culture of the day. The expressionist root discerned in Gaudí by the members of the German *Frühlicht* movement or the Dutch *Wendingen* in the second decade of the 20th century was a correct interpretation of the critical tension that made Gaudí in some ways a peripheral figure in relation to *Modernisme* as a whole, a figure characterized by a conception at once more complex and more contradictory than those of most artists of his generation. Not only because in Gaudí the model of boundless, continuous progress is opposed by the summons to tradition, but also because his work counters the new ethic of productive, conquering freedom with a defence of the pre-industrial organic order to the benefit of the principle of authority, the traditional social structure and the educative and moralizing character of art.

The situation of European architecture

The obsession of the most clear-sighted architects in 19th-century Europe was the search for their own identity. The question: "In what style should we construct the buildings of our age?" can be found over and over again in texts, treatises and the records of professional meetings, synthesizing the polemics aroused by the great changes inherent in contemporary industrial society.

This civilization had introduced a positive method for facing most questions: in dealing with any problem one endeavoured to consider all such results as past experience might offer, and then to arrange and analyse them in such a way as to obtain some solid, convincing knowledge from the operation. This, of course, was also the rule in architecture for 19th century architectural culture was of a positive nature. The authority of the classics was no longer accepted as indisputable doctrine, and from an empirical knowledge of the architecture of the past it could be shown that the architectural problems that had arisen through the centuries had been solved in very different ways. This meant that as a result of this research contemporary architecture seemed to be lost in a sea of doubts. Why was Greek architecture better than Muslim? Why had we followed the Renaissance-Classical tradition, forgetting all the positive aspects of medieval architecture? What were the comparative advantages of one and the other? What were the aspects that should be given priority when it came to choosing a solution based on the past: the constructive, the economic, the symbolic? These were some of the questions that constantly beset the architects of the 19th century; and it was exactly this type of problem, as we shall see, that Gaudí had to cope with.

European architecture at first found only one answer, which was that of eclecticism. There was no previous judgment that could determine the priority of any given historical tradition over another, nor could any absolute criterion decide what the style of the future should be — if it was to be supposed that any such style would be simply the continuation of one of the many styles of the past.

At all events this eclectic culture, which had all past styles, all traditions, unlimitedly at its disposal, established the first prerequisites for renewal and for the invention of an absolutely new style — which was at all times the ultimate aspiration of the architects of the day. They may not have known what this new way of giving shape to architecture would be like, but they did know that it could not consist in simply prolonging the results of the past. In establishing the inviability of any mere exploitation of tradition and history, the eclectic culture likewise established the need to transcend the traditions, mingling all their teachings afresh in a single crucible, from which would emerge the language of the new age — their own positive, scientific and industrial age.

Among all the experiments and proposals aimed at doing away with eclectic architecture, and with that aftertaste of Neoclassicism which was at bottom the real centre of that style, undoubtedly the strongest movement of all was the one that reappraised the possibilities offered by medieval architecture — particularly Gothic architecture. In France, in England, in Germany, in Italy and also in Spain, there was a powerful tendency that led architects to approach Gothic architecture with the conviction that in it were to be found the most satisfying teachings for solving the problems of contemporary architects.

Gothic architecture was seen above all else as the opposite of the classicist tradition. While the classical architects, from Brunelleschi to Quatremère de Quincy, had viewed Gothic architecture with horror as a positive sample-book of incongruencies, now, since the chief desideratum among many others was to demolish the smug security of the classicists, this view had to be diametrically reversed; that is to say, things had to be seen from the point of view of that architectural system with which the classicists had declared their utter incompatibility.

But the vindication of Gothic also had moral and even political connotations. Gothic was the style of European spirituality, which meant the recovery for architecture of a certain dimension of the sublime. Gothic architecture was an architecture with immediate roots in the religious and transcendental, and it was through these references that modern architecture might recover the lost values of its artistic feeling.

Pugin, for instance, believed that the only antidote architecture could provide for the materialism and spiritual impoverishment of modern man was that of its spirituality. Architecture, since it was a collective task, appeared to him as the manifestation of a social order which had existed in the past and which should now be restored.

On the one hand there was the idea of a collective, anonymous achievement, the result of collaboration by different craftsmen, each one with his own particular skill and knowledge, and this seemed to re-invent for architecture its character as a place for cooperation and honest, painstaking work.

The work of art could be thought of as a task to which each man contributed his particular skill and effort, one in which nobody set himself up as a solitary genius or a definitive authority. These ideals of work and collaboration were those of social reformism; and they were also the expression, in the context of art and architecture, of more profound aspirations which came from the architects' own view of society and from their critical attitude to the contemporary situation. This way of evaluating architectural work was clearly shared by Gaudí.

On the other hand, however, Gothic architecture also meant the reinforcement of the ideals of national cultures, so much more individual and authentic than the indiscriminate internationalism of the classicist language still maintained by the eclectic tradition.

Apart from the decline and fall of the *ancien régime*, the principal political feature of the 19th century in Europe was the formation of the national states. This formation, however, was not merely an affair of constitutions or geographical frontiers, but was also determined by linguistic, cultural and artistic peculiarities. In this sense Gothic art, and the medieval structural and stylistic traditions in general, may be seen as the source of differential positions. English Gothic, for instance, is a very different thing from the Gothic of northern Italy or southern Germany. For the social and cultural aspirations that characterized the nationalisms of the period, the restoration of this element of identity in contemporary art meant the possession of something that would identify the political project with the artistic results and with the very construction of the state. The interest aroused in 19th century Catalonia by the country's own tradition — the local Gothic and the technical and stylistic solutions that characterized it — was directly linked to that aspiration to a national identity which was fostered by the metropolitan culture of Barcelona. The Catalan character of Gaudí's architecture was emphasized from the very moment it first appeared, either by the architect himself or by the collaborators, critics and politicians who saw in it an evident example of how the originality of his work should be associated with the search for the vernacular and native in all fields of cultural creative activity.

Gaudí's work, however, was also a sharer in other yearnings characteristic of the European architecture of his time, yearnings which had their origin not so

Eugène Emmanuel Viollet-le-Duc: Construction in stone and cast iron. *Entretiens sur l'architecture,* Plate XXIII. Paris, 1864.

much in nationalistic or religious feelings as in his contemporaries' trust in the science and technology of their age as reliable guides in their search for the most suitable solutions to the problems of the day.

This insistence on finding the architecture best suited to the needs and resources of the new society meant that architects had to apply themselves to the critical study of the procedures used by the architectures of the past. A rationalistic attitude to the teachings of the past required that these teachings be subjected to criticism and, above all, reappraised in the light of the more precise knowledge now available from archaeology, history and the study of the resistance of materials and the statics of buildings.

The great master of this attitude was undoubtedly Eugène Emmanuel Viollet-le-Duc, an architect apparently devoted to archaeology and restoration, but one who made his studies of medieval French architecture a permanent reflection on the general problems of the architecture of his time.

He attempted to make a rational analysis of the way in which the different solutions actually worked in building, evaluating their safety and efficacy, as also the suitability of the materials employed to the form of the building; he set himself the problem of the building's final form and appearance, as in the result of the technical methods used in its construction: these were the basic preoccupations dealt with in this French architect's copious publications,

9

H. P. Berlage: Stock Exchange, Amsterdam. Contracting hall. 1903.

Hector Guimard: Canopy over the entrance to the Paris Metro. 1900.

which very soon found their way all over Europe and became quite familiar to Catalan architects in the closing years of the 19th century.

For Viollet-le-Duc the only way of arriving at a genuine architecture of his time was by advancing along the road of constructive rationality, from the choice of material to the particular solution of every technical detail. Beyond the forms offered by the past, this position represents a decided attitude to tradition which is assured by its own stock of technical and scientific knowledge. With the conviction that the methods used in the past for measuring the efficiency and exactitude of building had been vastly inferior to those available in their own time, the men who maintained this attitude were not afraid to manipulate the different traditions, reconsidering them and modifying them to whatever extent they found suitable, for the sake of a perfection for the achievement of which they put their trust in technical rationality as the ultimate justification of architectural form.

The fact that for Viollet-le-Duc in particular — as also for his disciple, Gaudí — it was from Gothic that 19th century architecture had the greatest lessons to learn, simply means that the reasons I have already mentioned (those concerning the interest aroused by Gaudí's architecture) were now reinforced by more timeless, and more purely rational, reasons, through which these architects believed that it was possible to go beyond eclecticism and attain to an architecture at once more authentic and better suited to the new era. For the architecture of modern times, Viollet-le-Duc means the establishment of critical and interpretative freedom with regard to the past. The various historical styles could no longer be seen as definitively closed and labelled repertories, regarding which the only possible option was to adopt them or leave them. This rational approach, on the contrary, implied the assurance of believing that by applying the critical faculties to the technical,

constructive and statical reasons behind what was already built, a sure road would be opened for the invention of the new architecture for which everybody was clamouring.

Gaudí, who never concealed his admiration for the ideas and studies developed by Viollet-le-Duc, and who is known to have possessed all the latter's most important works, was only one among many architects powerfully influenced by his way of thinking. More radical in some aspects, above all in the redesigning of the supporting structures of buildings, more traditional in others — for instance, in the limited use Gaudí made of the new materials and of the consequences deriving from those materials in the final form of the building. Nevertheless, the work of the Catalan master should not be seen as an isolated phenomenon, but as a variant of an overall process and one which is paralleled in other great European figures.

H. P. Berlage (1856-1934) in Amsterdam, Victor Horta (1861-1947) in Brussels, Anatole de Baudot (1834-1915) or Hector Guimard (1867-1942) in Paris, were also direct followers of the teachings of Viollet-le-Duc, and in all of them we find this freer approach to the design of the supporting structure of buildings and, consequently, to those buildings' ultimate shape.

In all of them we seem to detect, from the start, a habit of reflecting on the Gothic constructive system advocated by Viollet-le-Duc, the idea of an autonomous system in which the coherence between the form of the supporting structure and the final form

10

of the building seems to be the most important subject. To isolate the structural, designing it with a view to its utmost suitability to its material and to the requirements of stability, would appear to be the imperfect lesson that Gothic was to teach all of these men, the lesson which they were to take to more precise and refined stages, whether by using new materials — especially in the cases of Horta and Guimard, with their steel structures, or in the case of de Baudot and his incipient structures in reinforced concrete — or with traditional materials like brick and stone, as in the case of Gaudí or, partially, in that of Berlage.

In all of them, anyway, the modifications they initiated with regard to the stylistic codes established by historical architecture came from that same freedom to break away and redesign on the basis of a constructive and statical criticism of the solutions of the past. In all of them, too, there was the conviction that the progress of architecture was possible, and that it was possible by way of technological rationality in building.

Early years

Antoni Gaudí i Cornet was born in Reus (Tarragona) on 25 June 1852, and was the son of a boilermaker who came from a farming family established in the nearby village of Riudoms. The Gaudí family originally hailed from the south of France — from the Auvergne, to be more precise — and had emigrated to Catalonia in the 17th century, probably fleeing from religious persecution.

The future architect was the youngest in a family of five, most of whom died young, and his childhood and adolescence were spent Reus, where he had his secondary schooling at the local *Instituto*. His lively character and only fair-to-middling fondness for his school subjects were already evident in those early years. The marks he was given, both during his secondary education and later, when he was studying architecture, were not exactly those that denote a student who works carefully and systematically. On the contrary, his academic record reveals a decided character who devoted himself to what attracted him, nonchalantly ignoring anything that, for one reason or another, failed to arouse his interest. Familiar to us from those early years in Reus, moreover, is the plan he and his friend, Eduard Toda, formed for the restoration of the monastery of Poblet, at that time abandoned and in ruins. It was not simply that the buildings of the huge monastery excited a sort of tripper's interest when they visited the place in the summer of 1867; they actually made enthusiastic plans for its restoration, not simply as an exercise in archaeology but with a view to the revitalization of the monastery itself, envisaging a sort of industrial phalanstery within its precincts. During the final, lingering death throes of Romanticism in Catalonia, the ruins of Poblet were an almost inevitable element in the original vocation of the great architects of the period. Even before their careers began, Rogent, Domènech and Gaudí, among others, seem to have sought the encouragement of those noble medieval stones to persist in their vocation. One would say that the great Cistercian foundation, undoubtedly one of the most important works in the whole history of Catalonia, wove a peculiar sort of symbolic spell when it came to awakening the architectural vocations of those who wanted to produce a kind of architecture that would be at once universal and firmly rooted in its own native soil.

In 1873 Gaudí left his home for Barcelona and enrolled in the Provincial School of Architecture, where he was to find an atmosphere which, though indeed provincial, was also one of great enthusiasm, as exemplified in the roster of the first members of its faculty. The Barcelona School of Architecture was a very recent creation, having evolved out of the architecture class at the old "Academy of Noble Arts." But in this latest phase its character was transformed by the special attention paid to the technological and professional training of architects. Hitherto there had been only one school of architecture in Spain, that of Madrid, and the new foundation in Barcelona was to be, from this moment and for many years, the second school of architecture in the country.

The character of the school was conferred on it by two unmistakable constituent elements. On the one hand, a great faith in the technological training of architects, probably as a reaction against the lack of training of this kind in the earlier schools attached to the Academy. On the other hand, the contemporary yearning to transcend eclecticism by means of a scholarly and universalist training. Behind the teaching of Rogent, Serrallac, Torras, Vilaseca, Font, Villar, Rovira, Domènech i Montaner, etc., we can find very strong influences from the French and German schools; a vast amount of attention to historical culture, through all sorts of studies of the monuments of the past and their constructive, typological and ornamental possibilities. But we also find the very clear-sighted opinion that this historical culture was not an untouchable heritage but material available for projecting which could and should be used in accordance with certain functional, economic and technical criteria. The eclectic climate of these men's teaching was not incompatible with the positivism of attitudes which placed scientific truth above any other criterion. Yet it is a well-known fact that Gaudí, as a student, was not particularly attached to the school and the circles of the more influential teachers. Neither his academic record there nor anything in his subsequent attitude to the place gives us the idea of a student happily integrated in the prevailing scholastic discipline and order. On the contrary, he was always to think, in opposition to all book-learning or academic teaching, that one should at all times favour direct experience, personal work and fidelity to one's own impulses above all the conventions of the scholars.

Of his designs as a student only a few are known, the most interesting of which are those of a covered central courtyard for a building intended for the Provincial Council, an entrance gateway to a cemetery and an assembly hall for a university. The first of these shows the technical meticulousness with which the designs were executed and the precision with which he designed the divisions of the stone arches and columns or the elements supporting the metal roof over the courtyard. The most outstanding feature of the second design is the freedom with which certain historical themes are reinterpreted in a large-scale monumental work. A magnificent arch, gently emphasized and with a bossed intrados very much in the classicist idiom, is incorporated in a massive gateway crowned by a free, stepped interpretation of the Lombard-Romanesque arching, which on the sides is given a more orthodox form with the presence of buttresses dividing the surface of the wall. A huge double metal gate with a sloping brace, like those he was frequently to use throughout his professional career, was intended to close this Romantic gateway, which shows an even greater concern for the effects of the sublime than for the coherence of the details.

The design for a university assembly hall, which was a work presented for his final examination, is really a complex assemblage of architectural details of the most widely-varying provenance. On a hemispherical dome of classical cut, with a circular ambulatory of an Early Christian type, this design proposes a dazzling scheme of ornamentation, with elements of Mudéjar, Hispano-Moresque and Egyptian art, which seems to be the result of an accumulation of colourful, exotic details rather than the consequence of any clear, previously-decided stylistic idea.

At all events, Gaudí's interest in the School of Architecture seems to be of secondary importance in comparison with the apprenticeship he served throughout his student years as an assistant in different architectural practices in Barcelona.

Since his family was far from affluent, in order to eke out the allowance they gave him during his years as a student, Gaudí had to work for a number of different architects, in buildings by whom it is sometimes possible to detect traces of his early style. At the same time he was providing himself with specific experience and developing that taste for practical problems that was to be a constant throughout his professional career.

He collaborated with Joan Martorell, for instance, during the years in which that architect was working on the Convent of the Order of the Visitation in Barcelona (1882) and on the design (never carried out) of a Benedictine monastery for Villaricos, in the province of Almería. The taste for both Gothic and Mudéjar art in Martorell's work made an intense appeal to Gaudí, in whose earliest work as an independent architect this taste was to be revealed in very noticeable fashion.

Gaudí also worked for Francisco de Paula del Villar, a teacher at the school of architecture and an architect for the diocese of Barcelona. He was also the architect who first began the work on the church of the Sagrada Familia, which Gaudí was later to continue for the rest of his life. Gaudí was likewise del Villar's assistant on a job entailing an historicist approach: the Neo-Romanesque apse for the basilica in the Monastery of Montserrat. But perhaps the most fruitful of these student assistantships, both in the diversity of the work to be done and in the degree of freedom Gaudí seems to have been given in doing it, was the one he had in the office of the master builder Josep Fontserè i Mestres.

Though Fontserè was not an officially qualified architect, in 1869 he was commissioned to transform the precincts of the old citadel of Barcelona into a municipal park (now the Ciutadella Park) and to redesign the surrounding area. The landscaping, the great monumental cascade-fountain, the buildings, railings, walls and monuments were all entrusted to Fontserè, and Gaudí's contribution to much of this work is both evident and important. In the design of the great cistern for the operation of the cascade, in some of the monumental sculptures, in the grilles and cast-iron gates at the park entrances, Gaudí left his mark — still that of a novice, tyro, but by no means lacking in force or, above all, imagination. Some constants in Gaudí's career, such as the inscriptions and the use of motifs from nature in the ornamentation, or of airy plumes and elaborate sculptural motifs in the design of grilles and lamp-posts, made their first appearance in the work he did for Fontserè. The lively curiosity that led him to make use of everything, and to experiment with all sorts of solutions and motifs, is as it were foreshadowed in all this work he did in his student years, in which scholarly precision and conventionality seem to be opposed to the specific taste for the material and for the craftsman's work that forms it, in a direct approach to the trades that construct architecture piece by piece.

Quite a few of the first commissions Gaudí had to cope with when he qualified as an architect in 1877 were also of this particular kind, entailing close attention to the specific conditions of their execution.

The lamp-posts Gaudí designed for the Plaza Real in Barcelona in 1878 and the more ambitious 1881 designs for the lighting of the Sea Wall, or the furniture he designed for himself, the display cabinets for the Cumella house or the shrines and altars he was commissioned to do during those early professional years are all prodigies of accumulative arrangement of materials, symbols and design solutions.

From the very start of his career, too, we can see Gaudí's encyclopedic taste for using the most varying repertories of symbols: those of classicism, those of medieval heraldry, those of ecclesiastical symbology, those of nature taken realistically in its plant or animal forms. All these cases are often accumulated in complex systems of discordant scales, creating a sort of multiple approach to the object designed. This can be seen as a whole in the hierarchy of the principal components, but it can also be seen in the particular order of one or other of its parts and in the subdivision established by ornaments and adjuncts in a vast system of complex relationships. There is, of course, a certain degree of the *horror vacui* peculiar to the period — the Victorian passion for superimposing and multiplying motifs and techniques. But there is also a sensibility in which the macrocosmic and the microcosmic meet, which in any of the objects designed by him arouses an inexhaustible sensation of dilation and infinity produced by the endless mechanism of subdivision and hierarchy that is a constant in his work.

This whole complex world of forms, however, is neither gratuitous nor blandly reiterative, but always has a sound, tightknit formal structure, whether in the statical problems of support in furniture, altars or lamp-posts, in changes of materials or in the technical solutions of joining, soldering or dovetailing. In all those works he took considerable care not to conceal any irregularities of the design but to show quite openly the process of the piece's construction or assembly.

The graceful lamp-posts designed by Gaudí for the Sea Wall, with their height of twenty metres and their rich vocabulary of symbols and allusions, or the wooden architecture of the prie-dieu for the Marqués de Comillas' chapel — a heavy Gothic bracket on light column shafts — are among the many other works that show the young architect's boundless symbolic and constructive imagination.

Among these early works I should perhaps mention one in particular, on account of the specific problems of content created by the commission in itself. I refer to the complex of dwellings, industrial premises and social club which Gaudí designed and built for the Mataró Workers' Cooperative, an organization with which he had been in contact since his student days.

To my mind the principal interest of this work lies not so much in the quality of the design and the architecture as in the significance of an undertaking of this kind and in Gaudí's working on it.

Those who write on Gaudí usually emphasize his religiousness and his adhesion to the ideals of order maintained by his patrons: the Güells, Milàs, Bocabellas, Batllós and other such families. In doing so they sometimes even attempt to conceal any idea of a younger Gaudí, less closely connected with conservative circles and less militantly Catholic. The more dandified, agnostic Gaudí should not be ignored, even though this may have been nothing but a passing phase in the youth of a complex personality. But what helps us to explain this connection with the ideals of cooperative societies and his reading of socialist writers like Dacich, Monreau or Lavasceur, or his friendship with such notably secular characters as Ixart, Guimerà and the latter's colleague, Oliveras, is the fact that in Gaudí there was a sensitivity to intellectual and human conflicts which his work endeavoured to reflect at all times, and which cannot be hidden behind an image of pure sanctimoniousness. The image of Gaudí the mystic should be shown in all its force and passion. This passion was neither trivial nor purely theoretical, for it was alive to very specific problems and situations, and it represented an endeavour on Gaudí's part to understand and come to terms with the contradictions revealed by the culture and society of his age.

Eclecticism as an experiment

Some authors prefer to use the word "eclectic" only in speaking of Gaudí's first youthful period, when he produced the series of minor works we have been studying so far. But in my opinion the term "eclectic" should be extended, as regards Gaudí's work, to a much later date, somewhere around the turn of the century, for throughout the intervening period that work was still based to a considerable extent on references to codified historical styles. That there may have been periods of greater interest in the solutions of Moorish architecture or in those of Gothic architecture does not mean definitively that we must discount the fundamental eclecticism of the work then done by the young architect from Reus. The simultaneous or almost simultaneous references to, and use of, solutions from different historical sources are the characteristics of this architecture — the absolutely predominant note in which is, in any case, that of experiment. Gaudí's references to historical solutions are hardly ever literal in the sense of reproducing precisely measured models. On the contrary, they are nearly always reinterpretations of constructive, ornamental or functional features which are incorporated into his design without demanding any overall logic that would lead to a previously established form for the building.

In this regard I think I should add that in the work done between 1882 and 1904 it may be asserted that the overall approach to a building is frequently weaker than the effort that clearly went into the detailing and the solution of minor problems. The total conception of the buildings done during this period of eclectic experimentalism is frequently blurred by the strength of the constructive, structural or ornamental details, so that even in the more typologically convincing works, like the Palacio Güell, the School of the Teresian Nuns or Bellesguard, the parts of the building continue to overshadow the whole.

The analytical attention to such problems as architecture may create in its several aspects of light, colour, space, tectonics, etc. seems to loom larger,

Antoni Gaudí: Design for the Güell Cellars in Garraf (Barcelona). Elevation. 1882.

at all events, during a period in which the historic materials are subjected to the severe test of assembly and redesigning.

Gaudí's first commissions of a certain importance came to him during the 1880s. The Casa Vicens in the village of Gràcia outside Barcelona (1883-1885), the holiday villa called El Capricho on the Marqués de Comillas' estate near Comillas, Santander (1883-1885), and the building intended to house the gate lodge and stables of the Güell family's estate in Les Corts, at that time on the outskirts of Barcelona (1884-1887), together with the warehouse at Garraf, near Barcelona (1882), which were never built, form a series of parallel trials which were to reach their highest point in two works of greater architectural importance and lucidity within this group of buildings, works in which the predominant references seem to be those made to Arabic architecture. We refer to the buildings of the Palacio Güell in Barcelona (1886-1891) and to the Teresian College, also built in Barcelona (1888-1889). The Casa Vicens incorporates an enormous explosion of the imagination and a brilliant display of ideas, which were to continue being developed in subsequent works. In one aspect, these were the utilization of the building styles of the Mediterranean and Arab traditions, with a mingling of materials and of tiles placed on the exterior. On the other hand, we note the marvellous and careful finish imparted to the interiors, literally Nazarí in style in one case, such as that of the ceiling of *mucarnas* in the smoking room, whilst in other instances the wealth of detail of the carved and polychromed wood and the treatment of the floors and furniture give a fantastic and unreal air to the succession of spaces and outer rooms.

The gardens, the corridors enclosed by selected solutions of marquetry work, the use of variegated tiles to crown the tops of the buildings — all these give free rein to an exercise of the imagination which outdoes in its excess the iconographic sources from which it takes origin. El Capricho in Comillas has similar characteristics, although it is the outcome of a more limited programme. Its ground plan is irregular and irresolute, without too much attention to geometry, which is always overcome by the liveliness of the textures and materials employed. A cylindrical turret, like the shaft of a column, all clad with green ceramics, is set above a pavilion formed by four monolithic columns of vaguely Romanesque inspiration. The top resembles an enormous capital, formed by radially disposed stepped corbels, on which was installed an enclosed balcony, the dome of which is supported, in a typical Gaudí caprice, by extremely light metal columns, producing the effect of a solid mass which is held up almost in nothingness.

The porter's lodge and the stables of the Güell estate in Les Corts introduce in part the treatment of an enclosing wall with a covering of false mosaic, following a free interpretation of the Spanish Mudéjar tradition. However, the area for the stables is an experiment of another kind. Vaults partitioned

Antoni Gaudí: Casa Vicens, Barcelona. Ground floor. 1883.

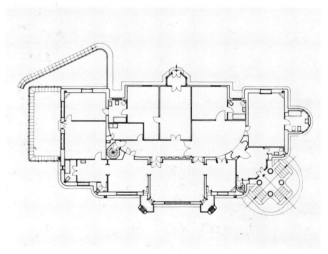

Antoni Gaudí: El Capricho, Comillas (Santander). Ground floor. 1883.

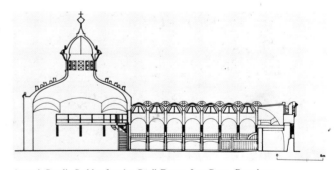

Antoni Gaudí: Stables for the Güell Estate, Les Corts, Barcelona. Longitudinal section. 1884.

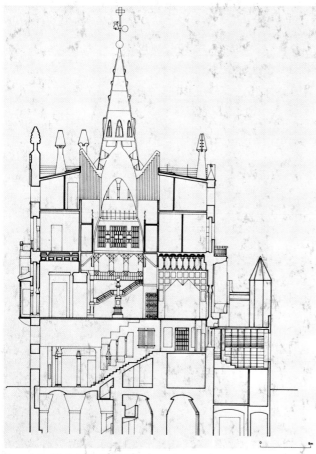

Antoni Gaudí: Palacio Güell, Barcelona. Cross section. 1886.

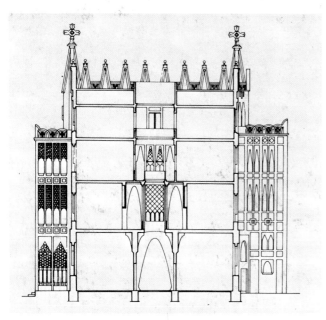

Antoni Gaudí: Teresian Convent School, Barcelona. Cross section. 1888.

off in a parabolic cross-section rest on arches which are a major light supply, these also parabolic, and all this structure is executed in brick. With this structure Gaudí developed a flexible system of providing a covering, economic and versatile, with which he had begun to experiment in the Casa Vicens, and which would continue to be characteristic of a multitude of his later buildings.

The Palacio Güell in Calle Conde del Asalto in Barcelona was to mean the creation of a plan which was more complex, but also more unified for the purposes of a large residential building. The building rose above a ground floor, which was founded on robust cylindrical pillars; it was almost square. At all levels it surrounded a central space and it was topped by a vault, parabolic in cross-section, with tiny star-shaped openings. The various outer rooms, such as salons, vestibules, galleries and living-rooms, were organized around this vertical space, with its potent feeling of centralization. The staircases and in general all the connecting spaces in this building are finished with special care, so that this results in what seems to be a deep penetration of some spaces into others, and in this way the precise delimitation of the various living-rooms is broken up. Furthermore the utilization in the corridors of breaks in continuity by partitions and of double courses of columns reinforces the spatial complexity of the building as a whole. Yet it is not correct to speak of fluidity, seeing that from the point of view of spaces, the only effects that are produced are major breaks in the closing-off of the surrounding areas and the formation of equivocal connections, which tend to complicate the possibility of transit. But for all that the design started off with limited technical planning methods, so that even the skill in detailing tended to negate the basic planning of this architecture. The wealth of ornamentation and the variety of registers of the types of colonnades, floorings, or flat ceilings which were proposed, did not prevent an understanding that the basic problem which was arguable about the building was the limit imposed by its individual spatial structure.

A similar problem, which presented itself less dramatically, but was solved with more clarity and sobriety, was that of the Teresian College, also located in Barcelona. Designed as a building of elongated rectangular form, with four floors and having a longitudinal axis for communication, this spatial theme became complicated from the moment when the circulation axis was split in two by a superimposed and subtle system of corridors formed by parabolic arcs, which, like parallel diaphragms, created an organized longitudinal form at the successive levels of the circulation space. An astute solution of the span needed for this central axis and a modified design for the openings in the upper part of the structure give this building incomparable qualities and a uniformity such as, perhaps, is not to be found in any other building by Gaudí.

From this moment on, we are able to see how the themes originating in Muslim architecture, which had so preoccupied Gaudí during this decade, slowly

Antoni Gaudí: Project for the Catholic Missions in Tangier. Elevation. 1892.

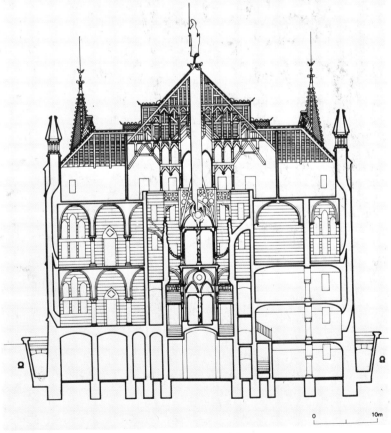

Antoni Gaudí: Episcopal Palace, Astorga (León). Cross section. 1887.

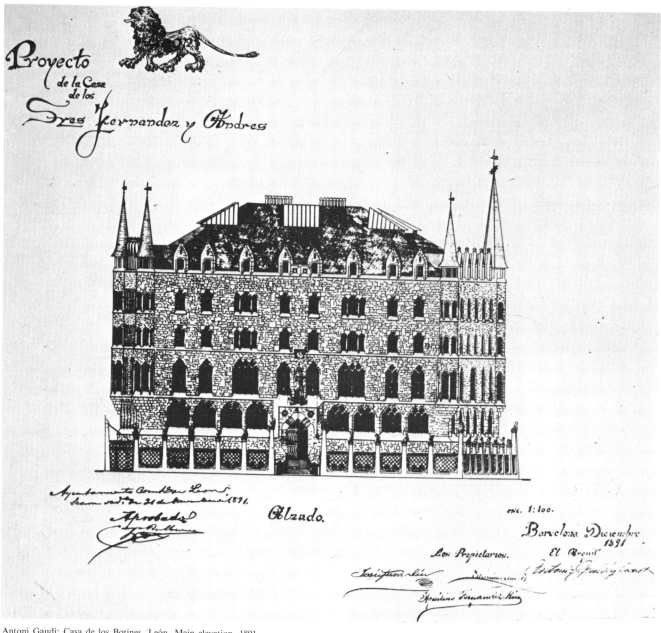

Antoni Gaudí: Casa de los Botines, León. Main elevation. 1891.

yielded to the reinterpretations, both personal and unrestrained, which Gaudí derived from Gothic architecture. The pinnacles of the Teresian College, the series of arches on the top story, or the system of diaphragmatic arcs, characteristic of non-ecclesiastical Gothic, came to dominate the final image of the building, despite the fact that walls of mixed materials, ceramics and lattice windows continue to remind us of the Mudéjar references which are the basis of many of his designs.

From the beginning of his work, Gaudí had in part surveyed the problematic aspects of the Gothic style, continually mentioning various elements or partial solutions. However, a more deliberate and global exploration of what might be called the Gothic system took place approximately during the decade of the 90s. The two works in León, the Episcopal Palace of Astorga (1887-1894), the Casa de los Botines of León (1891-1894), along with the Bellesguard building in Barcelona (1900-1902), and the project for the building of the Catholic Missions in Tangier

(1892-1893), are the most literally Gothic experiments which Gaudí carried out during this period of his life, a period which we have designated as experimental eclecticism. Of course one must add to these works, and to this period in time, the work which he had started in 1883 for the Expiatory Church of the Sagrada Familia. Gaudí went through a significant mental process when engaged on this unfinished work, which was a summary of all his architectural vicissitudes, since the project for this "Grand Temple" went through phases and varying periods, according to the way in which Gaudí's architectural personality matured and took form; thus, during a first stage it was very much academically Gothic, closely following the initial Neo-Gothic project of the pioneer of the Temple, Francisco de Paula del Villar, but it was to follow more personal and free interpretations of that expressive building system, which permitted a profound reflection about the scope and possibilities of the Gothic system, which would be so decisive for Gaudí's subsequent work.

18

Thus the initial elaboration of the Sagrada Familia and of the non-ecclesiastic Gothic buildings, mentioned above, may be considered to be the stage of his most explicit critical thought about the possibilities of utilizing the architecture of a determined period of history, just as in previous years he had come close to Arab and Mudéjar architecture.

Although its roof was not completed according to Gaudí's plan, the Episcopal Palace of Astorga stressed the theme of a central space, which was to organize the vertical circulation and the surrounding principal rooms in the form of a square story, topped on the corners by cylindrical towers, and by others which rose above the wings for the throne room, the chapel, the library and the reception salon. Despite the fact that few examples of it were built, this floor scheme was one of those most customarily put forward by Gaudí throughout his life, and in which there is most noted the aftereffects of the would-be academic philosophy of history as taught at that time in the schools of Europe. The symmetry in design, the standardized character of the multiple solutions for windows, colonnades, capitals, balustrades, buttresses, etc., a certain coarseness in the arrangement of the masonry made from white granite from Bierzo — these brought about a solution that was feeble enough for this castle, so closely allied to the copies of a new ground plan brought into fashion by the followers of Viollet-le-Duc.

The Fernández Andrés house, also called the Casa de los Botines in central León, has similar characteristics, although perhaps the nature of this building to accommodate every-day living obliged the architect to cut down on the treatment of the global mass of the structure, by means of a more customary and repetitive system of openings, superimposed floors and tops.

Yet if these two buildings can in some manner be understood as an exercise of trial-and-error with the language of the Gothic, the rebuilding of a country house on a site where there had existed a small and ancient rest villa, built by King Martín the Humane in the foothills of Tibidabo with views over the plain of Barcelona, may be seen as having a much more ambitious scope. Bellesguard is a building of approximately square design, flanked by a lofty tower with an enclosed viewing balcony, and topped by the characteristic crucifix of four arms which Gaudí so often put in place as the culminating point of his buildings. The Gothic touches in the façades, though allusive, are not literal but have a metaphoric nature, which is the result of a redesign in which neither the form of the material, nor its lightness, nor the proportions produce anything more than a parody of the historical forms re-introduced in the building.

As regards the interiors, these he executed with still more freedom. Certainly there are Gothic themes, but these may at best be referred to as being in parenthesis. His preoccupation with structure, as is evident in the attic, the main rooms, or in the semi-basement, or the resolution of the staircase, shows that he was continuing to think about the struc-

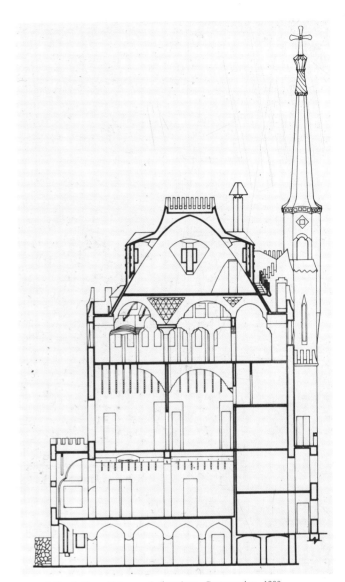

Antoni Gaudí: Torre Bellesguard, Barcelona. Cross section. 1900.

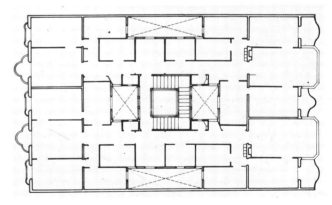

Antoni Gaudí: Casa Calvet, Barcelona. Standard floor plan. 1898.

tural problem involving free-standing colonnades, which he had extracted from the interpretation of the Gothic spirit put forward by Viollet-le-Duc. What happened was that this line of thought was continually becoming more personal, free and creative, and furthermore it did not constitute a mere eclectic imitation, but was an innovative experiment based on proposals derived from a definite historic architecture.

In this account of several periods of the history of architecture, it is necessary to point out the stimuli of invention and of planned solutions of an original nature, which were peculiar to the architecture of his era. Thus, in our opinion, as regards the thinking of Gaudí around the beginning of this century, it is necessary to consider and to add to the account the apartment house which Gaudí was to build for Pedro M. Calvet in the Calle de Caspe in Barcelona (1898-1904). The project originated in the usual type of organization of neighbourhood housing blocks in the Extension (Ensanche) of that time, which followed in the tracks of a well-established architectural idea of the period. This consisted of two apartment units on each floor, surrounding four open spaces for interior ventilation, with a double façade facing the street and the internal patio of the block.

Stylistically, this building corresponds, in terms of ornamentation, to the various baroque ideas which can be seen reinterpreted in the balconies and bay windows of the main façade, the use of helicoidal columns in the vestibule and the well of the main staircase, and the supple top of the façade with a double curvilinear gable end, which is certainly inspired by the baroque.

We must note here that basically the rear façade of the building is perhaps the most creative part, with no stylistic references from elsewhere; here Gaudí reinterpreted the customary solution of rear galleries using a more complex finish of a continuous line of small and large balconies so as to blend the light and make use of the spaces between the balconies. Actually this contribution began to constitute more than an ornamental re-creation of historical styles and it presented problems of re-examination of a type which not long afterwards would become more radical in the Casa Batlló (1904-1906) and the Casa Milà (1906-1910). But we have already pointed out that this first period in Gaudí of confrontation with historical styles is in fact an analytical and experimental era, but it was not as yet common for him to arrive at synthetic formulations; on the other hand the period was dominated by the drive to understand, prolong and go beyond an eclectic reception of historic tradition.

Several conclusions make it possible to describe the character of this first period of Gaudí's creations, all of them being in fact associated with a re-interpretation of style.

In the first place there is the breaking-up of the global composition so as to give more value to the fragments. It is important to indicate how, during this first era, despite its proximity to Gaudí's scholastic apprenticeship, his work is formed in overall composition in a manner quite distanced from the rules of academic composition. To be exact, Gaudí's ground plans, elevations and cross-sections, which for some reason are not abundant as documents, do not have the capacity to *explain* their art, as in academic architecture. It is the attention paid to the problems of individual parts, the splitting up of the edifice into a multitude of individual pieces, which characterize this first period. A break-up of the custom of dividing space into boxes, appropriate for an architecture of the masses, is also a first consequence of the same attitude towards space. Gaudí still had not formulated a plastic form for fluidity and continuity, but he had established the basis for this by means of alterations in the orthogonal wall construction, usual at that time for building problems such as he had to resolve. Breaking up the enclosed areas formed by the compartmentalization by walls was the result of the attention he paid, piece by piece, to structural problems, illumination and the textures of the finishes.

Furthermore, this stage of experimenting by Gaudí established a technique typical of modern thinking, that of distancing from what had gone before. We have seen that Gaudí's architecture in this period was made up of constant allusions to historic architecture, with re-creations of themes already codified and metaphors of forms long known. But this linguistic technique, which originates in an eclectic conception, according to which the character of the building can be created only by means of mechanisms of relationship, through which we refer back to established linguistic codes (such as may be the case for well-defined systems of style in archaeology and historiography), was used by Gaudí as a more subtle manipulation. He did not quote from it literally. He did not imitate it obediently. On the contrary there was a more perverse process of distancing, by which changes in scale, format, constructive solutions of arrangement and detailing do not refer directly to established sources, but there is interposed a barrier of novelty and change, which makes his language a constant stimulus to create the unexpected. Of course it was this aspect which subsequently fascinated the Surrealists when they came in contact with the work of Gaudí.

This distancing of meaning is related to another linguistic technique, typical of Gaudí's architecture, which appeared from the beginning and which is the third characteristic which we wish to point out. This aspect is the freedom of association of ideas which the architect made part of his work. We have already pointed out the lack of guide lines, which may be seen in his buildings from the moment of first planning. The particular point of academic architecture is that from the very beginning the order of events is to be left unchanged without surprises, so that the development of the building is to proceed along fixed lines. Now, on the contrary, this did not exist for Gaudí, who at no time whatever produced buildings in a style which had been guided by principles of coherence. Neither the form of the complex, nor references dominated by a certain style, nor the method of building eliminate the possibility of being surprised by brusque changes of theme, by the association of themes which seem separate, or by simple collage of iconographic materials emanating from various sources. In this aspect of Gaudí there is something which connects him with the most marked features of the Anglo-Saxon picturesque tradition, which is as much as to say, with one of the fundamental, perhaps the most fundamental, sources of modern sensibility. The creation of an aesthetic effect as a result of the free association of feelings was translated into architecture by a process of design in which nothing is determined beforehand and in which the means used may possibly involve surprise and psychological shock.

Finally, as a further observation of the characteristics evident in this era of Gaudí's experimental eclecticism, and which was to continue in later works, it is necessary to point out that the search for the essential in every problem stands out as a method of work characteristic of that architect.

Solutions to the conflicts about design which appear in any given work can be resolved by harmonizing them with other problems, with other exigencies which are involved in the development of the building. But there is another possibility, which is that in reacting to a conflict which appears as critical, and which may well be essential, all the stress may be laid on what is considered as happening by chance, and which may be relegated as not existing. In this period, this form of radicalism appeared in Gaudí in the design of furniture — that of the Palacio Güell or of the Casa Calvet — up to the point where emphasis on the structure of a basement, a staircase or a roof, or the redesign of a window or a turret come into conflict with the notion of coherence or of equilibrium, which has always been propounded by the classical tradition.

The 'Modernisme' Synthesis

In the work of Gaudí, the first decade of the 20th century was to coincide with a time of synthesis, which, although fragile, represented the culminating point of his work, and above all, of all his efforts to produce a new architecture.

Many critics have accepted with what is perhaps excessive benevolence this idea of producing a new architecture as put forward by Gaudí and many other architects of the time. Certainly during the last years of eclectic culture, the general clamour in Europe and America for a new style, for a language differing from those of historical origin, for an expression of the yearnings and changes of modern civilization, was almost constantly in evidence. Gaudí also participated in this universal desire, and in quite a few ways he was motivated by it. His disciples and followers certainly thought that Gaudí had achieved this, since his work constituted a fundamental contribution to this new art — Art Nouveau — of modern times.

The years which we are about to analyse are precisely those in which these hopes were cherished, and possibly they were the years during which was concocted the interpretation of a Modernista Gaudí, that is to say, of an architect who was contributing in a clear and positive way to modern building and self-expression. It is well-known that the term Modernisme meant in Catalonia what in other European cities was to be called Art Nouveau, Jugendstil, Sezession, Liberty, Floreale, etc. Gaudí's position within this cultural and aesthetic current, called Modernisme in Catalonia, is at most tangential. We cannot deny that he formed part of this broad movement, but it is no less certain that he consciously placed himself as one who was critical and reacting, as regards the progressive lay aestheticism to be found as the basic ideology of the most distinguished Modernistes.

In any case, however, once we have taken into account this peculiar affinity in some aspects, but rejection in others, in relation to the phenomenon of Modernisme, it must be said that if at any given time the affinities prevailed over the discrepancies, it was precisely during the years at the beginning of our century, perhaps when Modernisme in literature and painting had commenced to decline.

These were the years when there was a decisive change in public esteem of the figure and the work of Gaudí. Hitherto his work had been little appreciated and even rejected as being incomprehensible and extravagant. In Barcelona not even avant-garde circles and magazines seemed to pay much attention to him. This appreciation changed at the beginning of the century. Gaudí began to be interpreted by his disciples and critics as a genius; as if he were a genuine contribution which Catalan art and culture were making to world culture, and as having for this

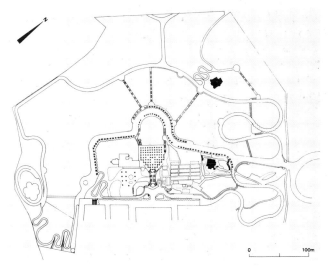

Antoni Gaudí: General layout of the Güell Park, on the slopes of the Montaña Pelada, Barcelona. Plan. 1900.

reason a value, not just respectable, but also worthy of praise and enthusiasm beyond the limits of questioning. With the development of Catalan politics, personages indigenous to local culture became the objects of special veneration. This was, *inter alia,* the case with Gaudí. He passed from rejection to praise, from incomprehension to being valued for his work, which was seen as being an essential contribution to contemporary artistic and architectural culture. Nowadays, almost a century later, our evaluation is less enthusiastic in terms of these ready reckoners of modernity and of the future, although perhaps it might be greater taking into account his originality and above all the intensity of the passion distilled by his works. If we do not believe overmuch in the modernity of Gaudí and in his character as a precursor of the architecture of the 20th century, the thing which impresses us abt ve all nowadays is the tremendous force and dramatic power innate in him, which were able to assimilate the contradictions of the architecture of his time.

After all it is certain that during the years which we are about to analyse, and despite a few of his works which were important and completed, Gaudí managed to condense a certain synthesis of the different problems which were on the point of discovery. This was a synthesis, which although it was unstable, fluid, changeable, managed to express a maturity and a sureness of touch which we do not find in previous eras. Although his own capacity as a critic was to lead him to make new re-examinations, it is certain that it was in these years that the originality of his language and its consonance with other parallel European experiments was made manifest in its clearest form.

The contact made by Eusebio Güell with the ideas of English social reformers was to influence the promotion of two private enterprise groups who combined for the construction of a garden suburb of residential type, the Parque Güell (1900-1914), and a workers' residential settlement in Santa Coloma de Cervelló (1890-1915). Güell regarded himself, along with other intellectuals, architects and politicians of the beginning of the century, as being one of the defenders of the ideas of Ebenezer Howard, and the result of this interest in the new form of understanding the growth of industrial cities as part of a new hegemony was the creation of the Social Museum (1909) and of the Civic Society for the Garden City (1912).

The plan for the Parque Güell as carried out by Gaudí consisted of the organization of a residential area for single family living units, isolated in a country estate on the Montaña Pelada, in the Tres Turons district of Barcelona. A total of 60 blocks of land, triangular in form and spread over the steep side of the mountain, were to make up the offer of land for building residences of good quality in a sunny area, with splendid views over the city and the sea in the background. Gaudí's work consisted of sketches of the street plan, the limits of the estate, and the building plan of services necessary for the proper functioning of this isolated residential nucleus.

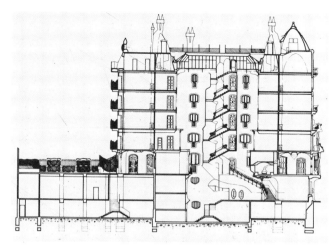

Antoni Gaudí: Casa Batlló, Barcelona. Longitudinal section. 1904.

The only buildings in the true sense of the word were the two on each side of the main entry to the Parque, which were to house the porter's lodge and the administration. For these purposes Gaudí designed two blocks of approximately circular ground plan, with their proportions made deliberately vertical, with roofs formed by curved surfaces, executed in vaults of brick sealed by rapid acting mortar, according to the traditional Catalan method. The administration block had in addition a pointed steeple, the most notable characteristic of which was that it was the first trial by Gaudí of the use of reinforced concrete incorporating steel rods. All this fantasy of roofs, like the coping of the top of the wall surrounding these buildings, in the middle of which one finds the entry gate, is covered with portions of broken ceramic (*trencadís*) which, set out over the complex geometrical surfaces of these volumes, give the buildings a showy and surprising look.

Gaudí went on to build accesses and outside staircases in the manner of an imaginative cascade and fountain, presided over by a mythological figure of a lizard. But perhaps the most interesting component is the hypostyle hall meant to be a local market for the use of the inhabitants of the park, and also the large lookout plaza, which formed the roof of the market.

The hypostyle hall consisted of a free interpretation of the classical theme of the telesterion, but with a completely subjective version of the classical column and the moulding of the friezes. In fact the spaces between the columns were covered over by domes partitioned off in the form of a spherical cap, which served as supports for the plaza above and as a receptacle for the water drained off from it, which was then deposited in a large cistern below the market, for use in the Parque Güell itself.

The most outstanding element of the plaza, apart from the spatial power of this large flat surface, which contrasted with the irregular slope of the mountain, was the balustrade and bench in combination, which set the limits of the plaza above the colonnade. Originating quite empirically from the ergonomic profile of a human in the seated position, to establish the type of cross-section, this bench ran a

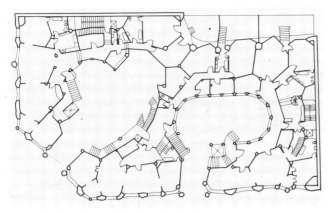

Antoni Gaudí: Casa Milà (La Pedrera), Barcelona. Ground floor. 1906.

serpentine course along the edge of the plaza forming meanders, corners and lesser spaces, intended as meeting-places for strollers and other users of this public area.

Together with its form, what turned out to be the most original part was the lavishness of its colouring, achieved, as were most of the design elements of the park, by covering its sinuous and capricious surfaces with broken glazed ceramics, forming a spectacular collage of fragments.

Finally we should observe the entire system of elevated viaducts, some sloping, which formed the network of communications of the Parque Güell, and which were to provide access to the plots of land. Stout inclined pillars, the bodies of which were continuous between arch, capital and base, and clad by stone hewn from the sites where they were placed, were built to form elegant arcades, above which ran the roadways. The exactitude of the calculation of the thrusts involved links up with the plastic fluidity innate in this complex, whose static outline, strength of form and ornamental finish combine in a unique and dynamic result. It is in the Parque Güell that references to historical styles have been abandoned by Gaudí, who now makes use of a language of which the continuity of the surfaces, the use of complex geometrical forms and the splendour of the colour and the finishes constitute the most specific aspect of the contribution of Gaudí to the *Modernista* blossoming of the turn of the century.

The rebuilding of the Casa Batlló, which Gaudí undertook during this same period (1904-1906), must be thought of in the same way. Its clear aim was to soften the rigidity of style which had become standard for the type of house found in the Ensanche of Barcelona. For this purpose, Gaudí modified the interior patio of the dwelling, giving it dynamism by the incorporation of a staircase with a tautly undulating outline, introducing an ascending linear motif that combined perfectly with the treatment of light in this vertical space. In effect, by means of a graduation in shade of the blue of the ceramic facing of this central patio, and a redesign of the windows which opened on to it, the sequence of vestibule-staircase-first floor-central patio was transformed into an ever-changing space, in which lines, colour and light

all contribute to an atmosphere of fantasy and wonder.

As regards the remodelling of the façade, Gaudí redesigned the openings, especially those of the ground and first floors, by means of enormous apertures formed by a support structure of stone, which left free (but as part of the structure) small window holes in a vaguely symmetrical arrangement. Above these forms, the remainder of the façade, undulating and faced with coloured ceramics and pieces of glass, provided one of the most subtle polychrome decorations of the era of *Modernisme,* all this being topped by a tower in the form of a floral bulb, with a tiled roof reminiscent of the spiny backbone of some mythological animal.

The enigmatic form of the balconies, the stained glass windows of the openings, the finish of the floors and ceilings, the furnishings which Gaudí designed for this house, all these things show how the architect commanded in his maturity a breadth of register that was perfectly capable of solving the problems which he himself had posed, by so freely rethinking the forms established by the architecture of the time. An intense yet abstract naturalism, evocative of floral, animal and geological motifs, and a capacity for exploiting these themes on a contrasting and variable scale, as well as providing in profusion a mode of creating a feeling of fragile instability, offer in the Casa Batlló a clear example of the degree of brilliance and sureness of touch possessed by Gaudí's work at this mature stage.

Yet perhaps the most ambitious metropolitan building, and the one which best demonstrates the Gaudí style — if we may call it such — during these years, was the house which from 1906 onwards was built for Rosario Milà in the centre of Barcelona, on the corner of the Paseo de Gracia and the Calle de Provenza.

Gaudí designed this building as a complex of spacious apartments, which were distributed from the corner façade and around patios of approximately circular shape, on both sides of the angular ground plan of the site. It seems that there was an initial idea of giving most of these patios a dimension such as would permit the construction of a helicoidal ramp, up which vehicles could ascend to service the different floors and apartments. Whether or not this was a lasting idea, the fact is that a design planning a structure around large patios was a fundamental modification of construction on corners, which up till then had been tried out as a solution proposed by Barcelona architects for the construction of corner buildings with bevelled angles, such as were typified by the designs of Cerdà for the Ensanche.

At this level of choice of type, as well as at levels of construction and ornament, it is clear that during these years Gaudí clearsightedly rejected all the established solutions, in an audacious exploration of different types of architectural structure.

The planimetric solution for the Casa Milà, popularly called "La Pedrera" (Stone Quarry), is a good example of this. The experiment is innovative even in its method of building. To the traditional

23

rectilinear structure of loadbearing walls, forming systems of parallel corridors, Gaudí opposed a system of free ground plan formed by a metal structure of pillars and trusses of girders. The structural solution of La Pedrera is complex because of the irregularity of its correlations, and because of the differences in load brought about by the interior patios, the façade, and the support needed for the basement, so that it can be used as a garage. In any case, the ways in which floors are divided into apartments are of such diversity and mobility as to have nothing in common with the rectilinear geometry which was traditional for the interior spaces of an apartment building. The clash of uneven and undulating planes, which form convex courses and spatial obstructions, is reinforced by a careful ornamentation of the ceilings and the floorings, executed with a skill and an imagination which are quite unique. As for the handling of the façade, it must be said that this is one of the most potent and perverse of all Gaudí's works. To propose the stone of Vilafranca, with its massiveness and density, coarsely smoothed down so that it involved inevitable projections of the surface, and to express in such a medium all this fluidity and dynamism, like the to and fro of a kind of surging wave, was undoubtedly an idea as potent as it was contradictory. It is certain that in this very contradiction one finds the attraction of his audacity; and further, the surprise and upset which is imposed on us by this façade is due to the fact that he has managed to master and mould a material which is physically and visually heavy with the aim of expressing precisely the opposite: lightness and ceaseless undulation. In any case, this premature surrealism which was to make such an appeal to the surrealists years later demonstrates, in this mannered technique of the contradictory use of forms and materials, a consummate example.

Finally we should point out that the roof too is original and unusual. Formed by a system coursing along the length of the façade of diaphragmatic and parabolic arcs, in brick, the resulting volume consists of a sort of attic, in which the internal space gives the impression of an inverted ship's framework, or the internal structure of some nameless animal of gigantic dimensions. It is precisely this fantastic suggestion of gigantic size or of something in a dream, which is seen once more in the solution of large chimneys which, like enormous sculptures, all different, form a top to the flat roof of the Casa Milà. Developing the experiment of complex geometrical surfaces which started in the pavilions of the Parque Güell, and utilizing in the same way a ceramic cladding of *trencadís* (ceramic fragments), the flat roof and the chimneys of La Pedrera represent in their lightness and fantasy a brilliant counterpoint to the darkness and dramatic quality of the stone façade.

We would also like to comment on another work of this period which we have labelled *Modernisme* synthesis. We refer to the work of restoration and re-adaptation of the choir and chancel of the Cathedral of Palma de Mallorca, which Gaudí with his assis-

tants and collaborators undertook between 1904 and 1914. The work consisted mostly of removing the choir, which was located in the centre of the main nave, so as to install it near the chancel, bringing it forward by one section of the nave, closer to the pulpit. In this way there was a transformation of the pulpit, the site and illumination of the main altar, the stained glass windows and some lateral altars, with some additional minor work. The work in Mallorca was not of major dimensions from the viewpoint of the volume of the work actually accomplished, but it showed a new sensitivity of perception of a historic structure, such as the great Gothic fabric of the Cathedral, and also a capacity to alter these venerable stone structures, without any undesirable carry-over from philosophies of history or ideas of archaeological reconstruction.

The work involved re-creating the clarity permitted by the perfection of the Gothic structure of this Cathedral, so much admired by Gaudí and his collaborators, both eliminating the choir and creating, by the use of lamps, a mobile suspended canopy and the new setting of the chancel, an ambience which had nothing in common with the traditional Gothic atmosphere, nor even with the later transformations which this had undergone.

In the work in the Cathedral of Palma de Mallorca the presence of collaborators was of no small importance. Joan Rubió and Josep Maria Jujol as architects, Josep Llimona and Joan Rebull as sculptors, not to mention stained glass makers, locksmiths and other artisans, contributed to the final result in a decisive way.

On this point we must note here a controversial question, about which it is difficult to come to definite conclusions. This is the matter of the relationship between Gaudí and his collaborators, and the extent of the contribution of the latter to the splendour and completeness of the architect's work. Certainly the technical ability of Rubió and the conscientious aid given by Berenguer are well recognized in some of the works. Yet the most disputed contribution, precisely because of the importance which one can sense that it had, was that of the architect Josep Maria Jujol. The period which we are discussing, that of the most complete *Modernisme* of Gaudí, coincided with the years of direct collaboration with Jujol, first as a student and then as a young qualified architect in Gaudí's studio. It is known that Jujol took a personal part in certain definite works, such as the bench surrounding the plaza of the Parque Güell, the ironwork of the balconies of the Casa Milà, and the ornamentation of the new choir in the Cathedral of Palma de Mallorca.

It is certain that later on, when Jujol went on working on his own account, these qualities and personal features were carried on, and they show his enormous capacity for plastic and colour creation, as well as his long-standing taste for organic undulating forms, which are always evoked by a working method which is taut and alive.

We are not trying to affirm that this period of *Modernisme* synthesis of Gaudí was in reality the work of Jujol, for that would be an enormous exaggeration. Yet what we do think certain is that the culmination of skill and driving energy seen in the work of Gaudí during those years cannot be evaluated without recognizing the major contribution which in the matter of ornamental finishes must be attributed to the ability and taste of his young assistant.

Our interpretation is that for Gaudí there was a cycle, which passed from experimental eclecticism in his early years to an architecture of destruction in his last works, with an intermediate period of equilibrium and synthesis, which we have denoted as being the most specifically *Modernista*. Thus the point which we wish to make very clear is that in our opinion, despite all the transformation and inversion, his architecture at that time was an exceptional synthesis of the assimilation of historical styles and the consummation of all his new departures towards the future and the end of his adventure in architecture.

Towards destruction

From 1908 onwards, Gaudí concentrated on very few works, which apart from the Sagrada Familia, which was to occupy the rest of his days, denote a certain radical change in attitudes that were already to be found in his earlier projects.

It is worth noting that in this final period of his life the architect did not re-create his own successes, not even the certainty and confidence of the *Modernista* synthesis, achieved in the years immediately preceding. On the contrary, it could be said that his work at this time was trying to carry on still further the possibilities of his discoveries, by means of works which ultimately proved impossible, but which by his inability to complete them were to become a symbol of the titanic force of the architecture of Gaudí.

It was precisely during these years that his work began to receive recognition beyond the local frontiers, so that both a commission for an early plan for a Grand Hotel in New York (1908), and the exhibition of his work in the *Société Nationale de Beaux Arts* in Paris in 1910, indicated the contradiction of a success in distant places, while the young *Noucentistes* (Men of the 1900s) in Barcelona began to distance themselves from the uncontrolled euphoria of the master from Reus.

The two most important works which these years brought forth were the hotel already mentioned, which never came to fruition, and the beginning of the building of the Chapel of the Colonia Güell, a project to which Gaudí devoted years of reflection and work, and of which the foundation stone was laid in 1908.

The characteristics of both these commissions displayed, in one way, a clear polarity. On one side, there was the grandiose American hotel, which could have taken Gaudí to the highest places in the international talent market. This would have been a triumph for the most attractive and post-eclectic aspect of Gaudí, as this existed at the beginning of the century, and it would have embodied all the decorative and symbolic display with which he approached it. Although the construction was halted dramatically in 1915, what was finally commenced was the church; its dimensions were of the usual kind and the needs of organic form and coherency were observed, with an almost biological conception of its structure.

The idea of a demonstration of large dimensions and a great display of decor seem to have been the attractions of an impossible voyage to America, which never came about, and which, if it had, would have substantially modified the final stages of Gaudí's life.

On the contrary, his work was limited to two churches, so that he devoted himself in the last years of his life almost totally to them. We shall leave to the end of this work an analysis of the Sagrada Familia, which in itself as a building is almost a summary of Gaudí's biography. On the other hand, in this section we shall analyse the other church of Gaudí, although it was not completed either; in it, the violence of his planning approach and the radical

Antoni Gaudí: Project for an hotel in New York. Cross section. 1908.

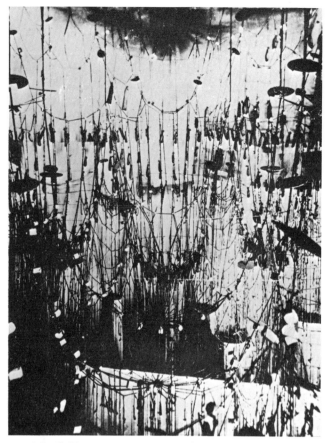

Antoni Gaudí: Photograph of the inverted scale model for the structure of the Chapel of the Colonia Güell. C. 1900.

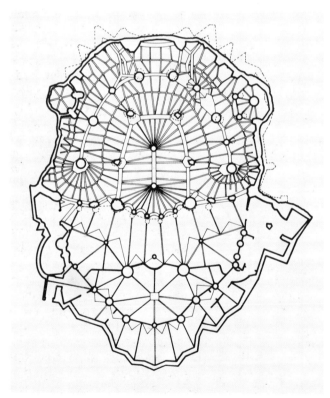

Antoni Gaudí: Crypt of the Chapel of the Colonia Güell, Santa Coloma de Cervelló (Barcelona). Floor plan of the structure. C. 1908.

way it was set out led Gaudí to what was actually a language of architectural destruction, in which the parts and the whole do not appear to be a reasoned process of composition, but on the contrary, the elements seem to be dispersed members, fragments only half planed into shape, which with indomitable force the architect tried to put together in opposition to a destructive hurricane which was leading to dislocation and a whirlwind of chaos.

Around 1908 there appeared to be a true contradiction in these two buildings: this was between the universal and metropolitan Gaudí who could have come into being, and the solipsist and elusive Gaudí, who was not to be fully realized either.

When in 1908, a New York multimillionaire chanced to visit Barcelona, he was greatly impressed when he went to see the Parque Güell and the Casa Milà, both recently finished. Since he was a good businessman, he translated the surprise which he had received from Gaudí's work into a concrete proposal; it was a matter of studying the possibilities of building a great hotel in the city of skyscrapers, which would challenge in its method of building, its decorative and symbolic splendour, the modern buildings then being erected in the great American metropolis. Gaudí's plan was like a great lay cathedral, and it made use, although turning them in another direction, of ideas which were already in preparation for his plans for churches.

The building, some three hundred metres in height, similar to the Eiffel Tower in Paris, or to the future Chrysler Building in New York, was to have had a circular ground plan, in the form of a monumental spindle, surrounded by similar forms on all sides. The result was a clustering and ascending complex, crowned with a powerful beacon in the shape of a star, full of symbolism and fantasy. The composition of the building carried to a further extent ideas which had appeared in the Casa Milà. The central nucleus of the great tower had superimposed on it a hall and six enormous dining rooms in various styles; five of them were in the indigenous styles of different parts of the world, and the sixth was to change according to the festivities to be held in it. A circular nave with parabolic arcades on two successive floors formed its upper part, above a large auditorium for several thousand spectators.

Gaudí seemed to adapt to American megalomania in this project, which never got beyond a simple sketch, since the further development of his ideas never came to completion. In any case it is worth noting that he showed a capacity, both in the discussions and the experiments which he had at that time planned, to respond to propositions as ostentatiously modern as this. Probably neither the technology nor the imagery fitted in with American aspirations of the time. It is certain that in this, his last attempt to plan in terms of an advanced industrial society, Gaudí's project, for all its grandeur, was a lost opportunity, a definite chance which would have profoundly changed his orientation and importance. With the vanishing of this impossible American dream, Gaudí remained confronted with his usual problems, in a

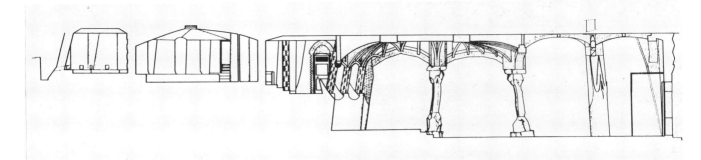

Antoni Gaudí: Crypt of the Chapel of the Colonia Güell, Santa Coloma de Cervelló (Barcelona). Longitudinal section. C. 1908.

society which was traditional and protobourgeois, under the double spell of a decaying historical architecture and a new architecture, which could no longer be expected to develop either from experimentalism in building, or from the naturalistic expressionism of its propositions.

The chapel for the Colonia Güell, on the other hand, was the monumental culmination of a vast operation undertaken by Eusebio Güell to endow his textile industry not only with a healthy and peaceful work force, in harmony between employers and workers and between manufacturing production and a natural way of life, but also presided over, as in an ancient classical city, by a temple situated in a small acropolis, close at hand, yet sufficiently distant, to watch over and keep in order the coherence of the complex.

According to Josep Ràfols, it seems that Gaudí had been working on the plans of this church since 1898, even though the construction did not begin until ten years later.

The first designs for this building were in structural coherence, leading the way to a complete definition of the form of the church. A critical survey of the Christian church and in particular of the Gothic cathedral, were not to be carried out in parts, in a fragmentary fashion, using redesign of arches and vaults, but had to lead to a total definition of the structure, with a three-dimensional system of the distribution of stresses. The method of reversed tensions which Gaudí used to define the form of the Colonia Güell is actually an experimental method that tried to make use of a well interconnected system, which at any moment, and in all its parts, would respond to modifications in weights or measures that might occur at any given point. This made the problem of the structure supporting the building seem an absolute priority. His construction of tension cables, with bags full of buckshot proportional to the loads at any given point, and sited so as to provide tension rather than equilibrium, was an ingenious empirical procedure for approximately measuring the distribution of forces in a static structure where everything produced compression. By this means Gaudí, who was putting forward the idea that it was possible to have a meticulous understanding of a complete structure, in which supporting and supported elements would be synonymous, limited himself to a method of working materials which was quite usual in the tradition of building with stone; this led, inevitably, to a complete self limitation in his experiments, and undoubtedly in a far from innovative direction.

We are familiar from photographs with his experiments with this maquette of inverted cable work; there are also photographs taken from various viewpoints with the aim of making available views of the future building and its outlines. Everything in this plan exudes organicism, despite the initial technical aspects of the planning. Notions of continuity and homogeneity of structure seem to comprise the essence of an idea which in actual construction would be handled with profound radicalism and austerity of expression.

In contrast, the ground plan of the church, as far as we know, was Gaudí's most fully completed effort to resolve in the form of a centralized design the main body of the building of a church. The idea of centralism in Gaudí's spaces was a theme which grew to be more insistent as his architecture matured. However, the centre which his forms of architecture needed to specify was not, according to academic tradition, a geometric site defined by abstract symmetry. On the contrary, his utilization of space is the result of an effort to aim programmes and structures in the direction of that cosmic and stable order which a centre has represented in almost all cultures. For Gaudí, the church had to be the site of centralism and of hierarchy. Centralism is certainly an idea which is constant throughout the long European classical tradition; it was revived at the dawn of the 20th century, when the intricate spaces of the arts of the Sezession, the transparencies of metal structures or the explosion outwards seen in the spaces proposed by Frank Lloyd Wright, were abolishing this archetype of composition. The hierarchy still implies the survival of the classical notion of space composed of reciprocally dependent structures; for these structures there is always a clear stratification of spatial values, according to which they are incorporated into a single mononuclear system.

It is worth noting that in the case of the Chapel of the Colonia Güell, these forms of hierarchy and centralism are not achieved by the simple application of a previously established geometrical or typological model, but by a titanic and involved effort at shaping anew these superimpositions; however, this is done by means of a polyvalent flow of incidental re-

27

ciprocal influences and organic inter-relationships, which the building seems to suggest by its analogy with a living organism. Yet in the Chapel of the Colonia Güell, what contrasts with these desires for organic unification of space by means of structural modelling is the design of the elements which are integrated into the actual building process.

In this phase of Gaudí's work there is a decided return to the elemental and the primitive. This primitivist movement should not surprise us, since it coincides culturally with what was being carried out by contemporary artists in other fields of art; this answered the need to find, in the primitive, roots which had existed previously in the historical diversification of styles. If, in one of Gaudí's first periods, we can identify an obvious eclecticism which had recourse to diverse sources in search of inspiration for his new architecture, and later on, a fluid synthesis in which stylistic moulds seem to disintegrate into a doughy material, capable of being shaped into endless continuities, now towards the end of his life, Gaudí in this creation of the Chapel of the Colonia Güell seems to return to the crudeness of gestures, to a rough sketch of basic forms and the elemental nature of the resources involved. The crypt built for the Colonia Güell is a brutal display of this elemental and primitive vocabulary. The columns have been reduced to the juxtaposition of three stones,

crudely hewn, which imitate base, shaft and capital schematically. The arches and domes demonstrate crudely the placing of their elements of construction, brick and stone, in a brutal exhibition of their normally hidden constructive elements. Lintels, doors and windows with capricious but basic forms are in reality explaining a construction which in its radical simplification is trying to take us back to monolithism and to the rudimentary actions of the task of building.

There is in the Colonia Güell, as in no other building by Gaudí, a major contrast of audacity and the interconnection of the structures, and the spatial result, which is fluid, mobile and fleeting, and furthermore one that is achieved with a limited and abstract repertory of building elements.

Thus the extreme severity and sophistication in the conception of the body of building represented by this edifice are finally expressed through a voluntary and ascetic primitivism, which moves from harshness to violence.

The effort of synthesis put into this church, as an important structure and as a system of space, is resolved by an abstract dismemberment of the architectural components, which with its crushed appearance of stonework joined by chance, manages to produce the paradox of a destructive construction.

The Church of the Sagrada Familia: a summary and discussion of the work of Gaudí

We have already pointed out that confidence in industrial progress and in the social changes produced by this new life was not shared by all sectors of opinion. In some conservative circles, the transformations being brought about, although they were leading at the same time to certain positive achievements, were also considered to be the cause of moral disorder, loss of traditional values and a social crisis.

Within this current of criticism, one must take into account the leadership of José María Bocabella, founder of a Spiritual Association of Devotees of St Joseph, which in 1881 had managed to accumulate sufficient funds to acquire an enormous building site, which occupied all of one block of Cerdà's Ensanche on the plain of Barcelona. They wanted to erect there a church dedicated to the exaltation of the figures of St Joseph and of the Holy Family, as symbols of the stability and ordered family life which were deemed to be basic pillars of the social order.

The proposal of this association was an ambitious one, inasmuch as it involved not only the construction of a large church in a new expansion area of the city, but also, in the minds of the promotors, this church was to be accompanied by schools, halls for meetings, and workshops which would allow the creation of a true social centre for the new metropolis. From the viewpoint of the Catholic religion,

the exaltation of the figure of St Joseph had grown throughout the 19th century, especially when he was seen as the patron of the movements which the Catholic Church was sponsoring as a reply to the growing lay and anti-clerical movements of workers. A clear traditionalism, combined with the exaltation of the family and of craft work, were the best defined characteristics of this ideological attitude.

However, this project of a church, which initially came into being with the idea of a site of commemoration, around which it was imagined that a social centre could be created, grew rapidly in the scope of its ambition when it was given the opportunity of becoming the cathedral of the new city. A neo-medievalist idea took form, and it pervaded the minds of all of the group of personalities who were promoting this church. In the same way in which the integrated medieval society was centred around a great building, which dominated the labours of the citizens, so also the new metropolis, which was growing almost limitlessly, should have its new centre in a great architectural monument, around which would be centred, in a visual and symbolic manner, the new society which would become established in its surroundings. At first it was called the Cathedral of the Poor, taking its name from the vein of compassion for poverty which ran through society at the turn of the century, but afterwards it was called the

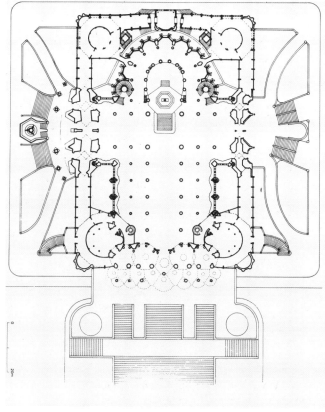

Antoni Gaudí: Church of the Sagrada Familia, Barcelona. Floor plan. C. 1906.

New Cathedral, openly accepting the idea that it was the whole of the new city that was to be endowed with a new centre and spiritual guide. The project of the Church of the Sagrada Familia (Holy Family) was to go on increasing in its ambition, not only from the architectural point of view, but also as a representative and social creation.

The commission was given originally to the architect of the diocese, Francisco de Paula del Villar, and the foundation stone of the new church was laid on St Joseph's Day, 1882. Del Villar's plan was academically Neo-Gothic and of much smaller dimensions than it was eventually to have in the hands of Gaudí. Not long after work began, when the excavation and formation of the foundations of the crypt were proceeding, disagreements occurred between the association and the architect, and these brought work to a halt and it was proposed that Del Villar should be replaced by another architect. Rather oddly, the new commission ended up with the young Gaudí, probably thanks to the mediation of Joan Martorell, the architect of the association, a prestigious figure and one well acquainted with both the dismissed architect and the future candidate, although he may have been influenced by the fact that Gaudí had been for some time a collaborator in Del Villar's studio.

In 1883, Gaudí at the age of thirty-one took charge of the work and began a revision in depth of the project which was to go on throughout his life. The first objective was to increase the dimensions of the building, taking as his guide the idea of a new

cathedral. Seemingly Gaudí also studied a change of location, since the site on which the edifice had been started did not allow either of a maximum use of the building allotment, or a more unusual and monumental arrangement of the church.

The town planning position of which Gaudí was thinking was that the church should constitute a sort of source of attraction, and in addition it should bring about a redesign of the urban plan of the new city, within its area of influence. A remodelling of the streets, the creation of avenues, an extension of the open spaces around the new church — all were the prime objective of Gaudí's search for a monumental design.

As far as a programme went, the type of church proposed started off with a model of the Gothic ground-plan for a basilica, with five naves, a transept and a wide apse, with the peculiarity that the entire building was surrounded by an ambulatory, which was to be called the cloister, even though this was a rather strange version of this type of space, which is meant to be organized around an empty space and not precisely around the mass of a cathedral.

However, the most eye-catching aspect of Gaudí's concept was undoubtedly the vertical development which was proposed for the Church. Eighteen pointed towers were to surround the structure, linked by the system of naves and exterior spaces. Taking up once more a theme characteristic of all his work — an interest in vertical elements and spaces — Gaudí proposed for the Sagrada Familia an authentic apotheosis of pinnacles and towers of an imposing height, conceived undoubtedly as challenging beacons which were to soar far above the uniform landscape of terraces and roofs of the city.

Yet the programme for the church was also a complex iconological one, in which the cathedral took part as a complex system of symbolisms and a visual explanation of the mysteries of the faith.

At that time Gaudí was taking part in the general movement of the European Catholic world in favour of a renovation of the liturgy, concerning which there were in Catalonia numerous adepts and students. To re-create the language of the symbolic forms, so as to revitalize the communication which could be offered by religious objects — this was the end pursued. And so it was to be in the new church of the Sagrada Familia. What happened in this case was that both in the use of symbols and in the proposal for a new liturgical organization for the Church, Gaudí demonstrated his accumulative sensitivity, which was both complex and excessive. The iconographic programme for the Sagrada Familia was an enormously diversified system of numbers, ciphers and symbols, expressing a multitude of doctrines which were but little used in Catholic teachings of the time. The three façades of the church were representations of the three culminating moments of the life of Christ and of the Church: birth, death, and resurrection. The pointed towers were the symbolism of the exaltation of the twelve apostles, the four evangelists, the Virgin Mary, and Christ himself,

First general view of the Church of the Sagrada Familia, published, after a drawing done in 1906 by the architect Joan Rubió i Bellver, Gaudí's assistant.

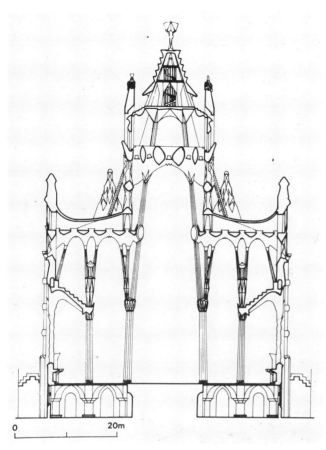

Antoni Gaudí: Church of the Sagrada Familia, Barcelona. Cross section of the naves. C. 1914.

Facsimile of one of Gaudí's drawings made by J. Matamala, showing the arrangement of the future Gloria portal of the Church of the Sagrada Familia.

exemplarized by the central and highest pinnacle. The lateral chapels were the symbol of baptism and of penitence, of the theological virtues and of the sorrows and joys of the patriarch, St Joseph.

But the use of allegory and of symbols is not evoked merely by the global conception of the building. The fascination which is now exercised on us by the portions constructed by Gaudí is brought about by the multitude of allusions at all levels. Geometrical symbols, animals and plants, figures in relief or in sculpture — all of these form part of a vertiginous panorama which passes in front of the astonished gaze of anyone who approaches this complex edifice, conceived as an immense catechism which can speak.

In this regard it is worth noting that the level of study of the technical rationale, which so preoccupied Gaudí, is no more than the first rung of the overall conception of the building, in which, as in some microscopic vision, the animate and the inanimate join only to unfold as in a permanent discourse.

The technical-constructive will power which Gaudí had to develop for such buildings is recalled here, as a distinct and finally dominating objective, that is to say, allegory. All the figurative reality of the fabric of the church was to be an explanation and an echo of a vision of the natural and supernatural order of things, which Gaudí wished to propound on the basis of Catholicism. However, these considerations should not conceal another aspect characteristic of the process of definition of this edifice, which is

transformation in time. Given that his project came into being from the beginning as a transformation, in reality the architectural project of the Sagrada Familia was at any given moment being subjected to a permanent review.

Certainly Gaudí thought that this church would summarize the whole of the investigations and findings of his entire career as an architect. In the classical manner, he thought that the architecture of the church was the culmination of the monumental style, and furthermore, the final synthesis of everything architectural. With a clear distancing from modern architecture, which arose from a thematic indifference to architectural problems, and thinking that there was a single code for composition and aesthetics which could handle any problem — from the drawing board to the city — for Gaudí, on the other hand, the church and its architecture continued to be a summary of all his experience and the site on which technical or geometrical findings were to be surpassed by a transcendent conception of this work of art.

For this reason it is not easy in the case of the Sagrada Familia to separate his technical and stylistic elaboration from the total objective of the building, which puts together and transcends particular problems.

In any case, this work, which was to continue long after his death, shows very clearly the stages of maturing which took place during Gaudí's life

31

and which we have been analysing throughout these pages.

During the first period, from 1883 to 1893, Gaudí introduced changes in planning which foreshadowed the blossoming of the idea. But in his working on the continuation of the crypt, commenced by Del Villar, and the beginning of the apse, he showed himself cautious in use of the Gothic repertory, which he still did not dare to criticize openly, and in which he merely introduced surprising changes, by way of ornaments of a naturalistic type.

From 1891 until approximately 1900, Gaudí worked on the construction of the Façade of the Nativity. Just as with the eclectic experimenting of that time on other buildings, the dominating characteristic of this part of the church is profusion. Re-design of the Gothic elements in the interior elevation, and experiments with ornamentation, sculpture, and symbolism on the exterior part of the façade seem to indicate to us the sort of preoccupation which inspired the architect at this time.

The years which we have called those of *Modernisme* synthesis correspond in his work to his overall definition of a building. These were the years of the first decade of this century, during which a greater geometrical abstraction, a determined exploration of curved surfaces, and in general, a free and uninhibited use of any style, allowed him to make just as great an advance in his overall definition of the project, his first drawings of which were published in 1905, as in the structural handling of the solutions of the roof of the church and of the towers.

The process of reappraisal and re-elaboration of Gothic architecture which we have mentioned in commenting on the project for the Chapel of the Colonia Güell came to fulfilment in the detailed study of the cross-section of the church. An initial estrangement from canonical Gothic led first of all to a naturalism of plant-like type, in which it was possible to assume in a flexible form the technical reasoning of structural continuity between arches and columns, the inclination of the supports, and in general, the three-dimensional deployment of structural arborescence.

For all that, it was not to be a satisfactory time for Gaudí, who, during the last period of his life, when he was absorbed almost totally in the problems of this work, would come back time and time again to seek solutions which were geometrically more purified, yet clearly more abstract and brutal.

The return to essentials, which can be detected in his final works, appears with all its force in the last studies still extant, and in the many ideas in the process of being worked out which still remained on his desk at the time of his death.

The sudden cutting-off of Gaudí's life is, in this way, a symbol of the fate of all his work, and in a very particular way of that unfinished work which is the Sagrada Familia.

Gaudí's work finished brusquely and suddenly, but it bore in its own origin the cause of its lack of viability, which does not diminish his grandeur by one iota.

It is surprising to find that those who consider themselves to be the direct heirs of Gaudí have hoped to show that continuity of his teachings was possible, and have tried to create a genuine school based on the master's work, accepting what may well be one of the hypotheses in his ideas which can most readily be given a date. The materialist positivism of the 19th century put forward an idea, according to which constructive rationalism in architecture was the road by which one arrived at full artistic creativeness. However, this conception brings with it the limitation that one must submit artistic creation to the narrow limits imposed by building, and further, to a method of building conceived on the basis of traditional materials and traditional systems of using them, in terms of their resistance to compression.

Fortunately Gaudí never stopped at the level of these problems, and he created a creative and imaginative concept of architecture, in terms of his time, with the romantic confidence of an individual genius, and with the subjectivism appropriate to a century which made experiment a pathway to creativeness and permanent change.

It is useless to recall that the cathedrals of former times were built over a period of centuries, when building methods and the anonymity of the builders introduced no changes from generation to generation. Yet today, despite a much greater discipline than in the past, when Gothic buildings were finished with baroque altarpieces and porches, we find ourselves in a situation of change in which the disappearance of the architect of a building often proves an irremediable loss. Continuation of the Sagrada Familia by the successors of Gaudí assumes at the very least a lack of understanding of the conceptual changes which our times have brought about in architecture, and which, for better or for worse, connect works intimately with the genius of their authors.

The architectural adventure of Gaudí is fundamentally a personal and even autobiographical one, though he relied on a substantial number of assistants, craftsmen and artists, who made the splendour of his works possible.

Yet in another way, his work, impressive and singular though it is, was built during the complex decline of the 19th-century dream of creating a new style for the society of that time, by means of an architecture which would still be the offspring of ancient monumental styles. There are too many contradictions to permit one to think of Gaudí as the first modern architect and a founder of the new rationalism of our era.

On the contrary, what the work of Gaudí reveals to us, in its declining grandeur, is the permanent effort he made to understand himself and to understand the place and the time in which he lived.

The fact that the work of Gaudí is contradictory, not even permitting of confident apprentices to succeed him, is in the last analysis the explanation of his intense pathos and of his hesitant humanity.

Chronological Summary

1852. Antoni Gaudí i Cornet is born in Reus on 25 June.

1873-1878. He begins his studies at the School of Architecture in Barcelona, obtaining his degree on 15 March, 1878. During these years, he works with the architects Joan Martorell, Francisco de Paula del Villar, and with the building supervisor, Josep Fontseré.

1878. Lampposts for the Plaza Real in Barcelona. Housing units and workshops for the Workers' Cooperative in Mataró, Barcelona.

1881. Project for the Sea Wall in Barcelona. Not built.

1882. Project for warehouses for Eusebio Güell, in Garraf, Barcelona. Not built.

1883. He begins the housing project for Don Manuel Vicens in the Calle de Carolinas, 24-26, Barcelona.

House for the Marquis de Comillas, in Comillas, Santander, known as "El Capricho".

1884. He receives the commission to continue work on the Expiatory Church of the Sagrada Familia, commenced by the architect Francisco de Paula del Villar.

Stables in Les Corts in Barcelona, for Güell.

1886. Project of a palace for Don Eusebio Güell in the Carrer Nou de la Rambla, in Barcelona.

1887. Project for the Episcopal Palace of Astorga, in León.

1888. Teresian College in Barcelona.

1890. He commences work on the Colonia Güell, in Santa Coloma de Cervelló, in Barcelona.

1891. House "De los Botines" in León.

1892. Project for the Catholic Missions in Tangier. Not built.

1898. Casa Calvet in Calle Caspe, 48, Barcelona.

1900. Country House, Torre Bellesguard, in Barcelona.

Start of work for the Parque Güell on the Montaña Pelada in Barcelona.

1904. Alterations to the interior of the Cathedral of Palma de Mallorca.

Remodelling of the Casa Batlló in the Paseo de Gracia in Barcelona.

1906. He begins the project for the Casa Milà ("La Pedrera"), in Barcelona.

1908. Project for a hotel in New York. Not built.

1926. Gaudí dies on 10 June in the Santa Cruz Hospital, in Barcelona, after being knocked down by a tramcar.

Bibliography

The bibliography about Gaudí is extraordinarily abundant, and it has been studied exhaustively by Professor George R. Collins in his Bibliography of Antonio Gaudí and the Catalan Movement, 1870-1930, Charlottesville, 1973. The following basic works may be suggested as a guide:

BASSEGODA NONELL, Juan: *Antonio Gaudí. Vida y Arquitectura.* Caja de Ahorros de la Diputación Provincial de Tarragona, Tarragona, 1977.

BERGÓS, Joan: *Antoni Gaudí: L'home i l'obra.* Ed. Ariel, Barcelona, 1954.

BOHIGAS, Oriol: *Arquitectura Modernista.* Ed. Lumen, Barcelona, 1968.

CASANELLAS, Enric: *Nueva Visión de Gaudí.* Ed. Polígrafa, Barcelona, 1965.

CIRICI I PELLICER, Alexandre: *El arte modernista catalán.* Ed. Aymà, Barcelona, 1951.

CIRLOT, Juan Eduardo: *El arte de Gaudí.* Ed. Omega, Barcelona, 1950.

COLLINS, George R.: *Antonio Gaudí.* Braziller, New York, 1960.

COLLINS, George R. & BASSEGODA NONELL, Juan: *The designs and drawings of Antonio Gaudí.* Princeton University Press, Princeton, 1982.

DALISI, Riccardo: *Gaudí: Furniture and Objects.* Barron, 1980.

FLORES, Carlos: *Gaudí, Jujol y el modernismo catalán.* Ed. Aguilar, Madrid, 1982.

MARTINELL, César: *Gaudinismo.* Amigos de Gaudí, Barcelona, 1954.

Gaudí: His Life, His Theories, His Work. MIT, Cambridge, Mass., 1975.

MOWER, David: *Gaudí.* Hippochrene Books, 1977.

PANE, Roberto: *Gaudí.* Edizioni di Comunità, Milan, 1964.

PERUCHO, Joan: *Gaudí: una arquitectura de anticipación.* Ed. Polígrafa, Barcelona, 1967.

PREVOST, Clovis & DESCHARNES, Robert: *Gaudí: The Visionary.* Viking Press, New York, 1982.

RÀFOLS, Josep Francesc & FOLGUERA, Francesc: *Gaudí.* Ed. Canosa, Barcelona, 1929.

SERT, Josep Lluís & SWEENEY, J. J.: *Antoni Gaudí.* F. A. Praeger, New York, 1961.

TARRAGÓ, Salvador: *Gaudí.* Ed. El Escudo de Oro, Barcelona, 1977.

Student works

Gaudí studied architecture between 1873 and 1878, and carried out numerous and varied types of work for his various academic subjects. We have come across a good number of these by consulting the archives of the present-day Escuela Técnica Superior de Arquitectura de Barcelona (E.T.S.A.B.)

1. Project for a covered patio for the Diputación Provincial de Barcelona (Provincial Government Offices). Detail in water-colour, scale 1/25. Archives of the E.T.S.A.B., 1876.

2. Project for a covered patio for the Diputación Provincial of Barcelona. Published by Ràfols in 1929. 1876.

3. Project for a cemetery gateway. Published by Ràfols in 1929 and destroyed in 1936.

4. Project for final examinations. Assembly hall for a university. Archives of the E.T.S.A.B. Section in water-colour, scale 1/100, 1877.

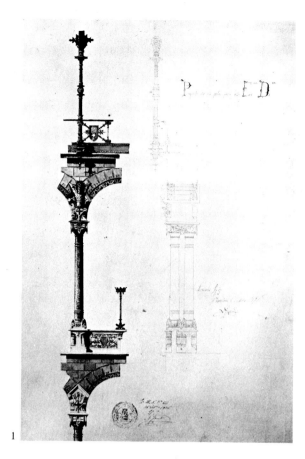

1

2

3

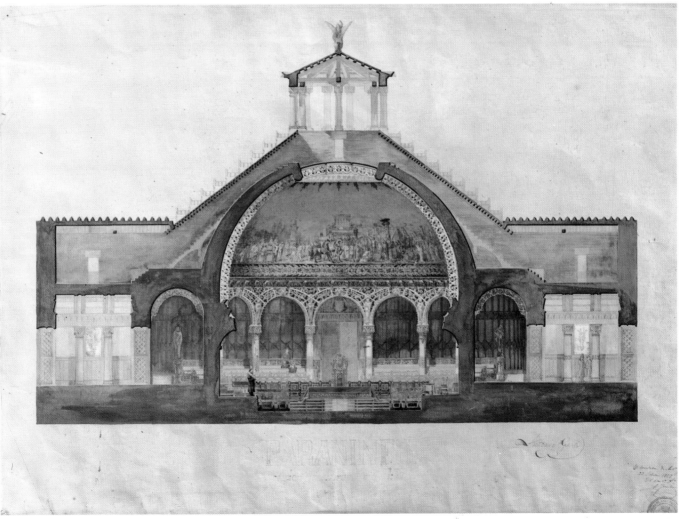

4

First professional works

During his first years as an architect Gaudí carried out a notable number of designs and small projects both for house furnishings and for small-scale street furniture. His participation in the complex of housing and other buildings for the Workers' Cooperative of Mataró is particularly important. 1878-1883.

5

6

5. Project for lighting for the Sea Wall in Barcelona, 1881.

6. Lanterns on the railings of the Parque de la Ciudadela, carried out during the period when he was assistant to the Superintendent of Works, J. Fontserè. Circa 1876.

7. Lamp-posts for the Plaza Real in Barcelona. 1878.

8. Project for a Club for the Workers' Cooperative of Mataró. Elevation, 1883.

9-10. Interior for the industrial plant of the Workers' Cooperative of Mataró, with convex wooden frames forming parabolic arches. Mataró, Barcelona, 1883.

Sociedad cooperativa "LA OBI

Fachada al Jardin   Escala-

7

8

9

10

Casa Vicens

A building constructed for Don Manuel Vicens
Montaner in the Calle de las Carolinas, in the
Gracia quarter of Barcelona, between 1883 and
1885. The building was extended in 1925 by the
architect J. B. Serra Martínez and the garden was
later to be ruined by the construction of a house
next door.

11

12

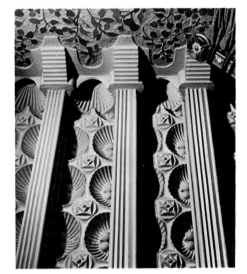

13

14

15

11. Casa Vicens, Barcelona. A general view from the Calle de las Carolinas.

12. Casa Vicens. Interior of the dining room and the "aviary."

13. Detail of the ornamentation of the dining room ceiling.

14. Detail of the main façade with tile facings.

15. Structure of complex brickwork in the solution of the turrets on the corners.

The villa El Capricho
in Comillas, Santander

This was built between 1883 and 1885 for Don Máximo Díaz de Quijano in the vicinity of the Palace of the Marquis de Comillas. The work was directed by Gaudí's assistant, Cristóbal Cascante.

16. General view of the building and the turret.
17. Detail of the tile facing of the turret.
18. Detail of a large window and a corner balcony.
19. Detail of the entry portico and the base of the turret.

18

17

19

Güell Pavilions

The Güell family owned a large country house in
the environs of the city of Barcelona, in what is
now the Les Corts quarter. In 1883 they
commissioned Gaudí to design a wall for this
property, some of the gates and two buildings
intended to be the porter's lodge and stables,
located at the main entrance of the property.

20

20. The cupola of the stable block, seen from the main gate.

21. Detail of the finish of the exterior walls, executed in moulded plaster.

21

22

22. Metal gate "of the Dragon" at the main entrance.

23. Detail of the head of the Dragon, carried out in wrought iron.

24. Detail of the flooring of the circular stable yard, with the monogram "G" of the Güell family.

25. Interior of the stables, which now house the Gaudí Chair of the E.T.S.A.B.

23

24

25

School of the Teresian Nuns

This building, considered modest in terms of the
available financial resources, was constructed
between 1888 and 1890, as a school and residence
for the Congregation of Teresian Nuns in the Sant
Gervasi quarter of Barcelona.

26. General view.

27. Detail of the wrought-iron entrance gate.

28. Ornamental brickwork finials and detail of the lattice windows above the main entrance.

27

28

29

29. Central vestibule of the building with lateral and central lighting.

30. Gallery on the first floor.

31. Diaphragmatic arches of brick, in parabolic form, in the upper galleries.

Palacio Güell

This mansion was built between 1886 and 1889 in the Carrer Nou de la Rambla in Barcelona, on a site formerly occupied by three old houses. The building was made up of a total of six different levels, from the basement intended for carriages to the upper story under the roof, with its phantasmagorical forest of chimneys of capricious forms and colours.

32. Main façade.

33. Coat of arms, placed in the curvilinear triangle above the arches of the main entrance, and made of wrought iron.

34. Detail of the wrought iron of the entrance grille.

35. Wrought iron in the upper part of the arches of the main entrance.

36. Bay window with wooden lattice in the rear façade.

33

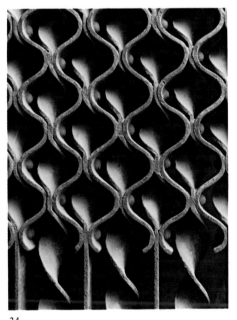

34

35

36

37

37. Support columns for the first floor, in the basement.
38. Brickwork on the descending ramp and columns in the basement.
39. Wood and iron coffered ceiling in the visitors' room.
40. Detail of a capital in stone and wrought iron.
41. The space of the central drawing room from the galleries of the mezzanine.
42. Corner of the central drawing room.

38

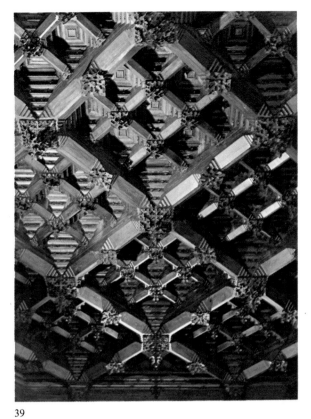

39

40

41

42

43

43. Interior lattice in wood and wrought iron.
44. Parabolic dome above the central drawing room.
45. Parabolic arches in the gallery at the main façade.

44

45

46. Roof terrace of the Palacio.
47. Detail of the tops of the chimneys.
48. Exterior of the dome above the central drawing room.
49. Detail of the ceramic-fragment facing on the chimneys.

46

47

Episcopal Palace of Astorga

Bishop J. B. Grau commissioned this new episcopal palace in 1887, dismissing Gaudí as director of works in 1893; this was the reason for the delay in termination until the second decade of this century, and for the introduction of modifications, especially in the roof, by the new director of works.

50. View of the rear portion of the building, which contains the chapel.
51. View of the main façade.
52. Detail of the splayed arches of the entry porch.
53. Detail of the arches and pillars of the chapel.
54. Arches faced with coloured ceramics, in the apse of the chapel.

50

51

52

53

54

The Casa Fernández-Andrés ("Casa de los Botines")

This is a large building in the centre of the city of León, of an approximately rectangular form, and designed to be the main residence of its owners, with other apartments which were to be let.

55. General view of the building.

56. Detail of the sculpture of St George, the work of L. Matamala.

57. Turret on one corner, with a slate roof.

58. Detail of the treatment of the wall, large windows and top of the building.

56

57

58

Bellesguard

This building, designed by Gaudí for the Figueras family, was erected on the same site on which during the fifteenth century King Martín I, (the Humane), had built a small retreat, far from the city, and dominating most of the plain of Barcelona. Building work was to continue until 1903, and various minor constructions were introduced at a later date by Gaudí's assistant, Domingo Sugranyes.

59. Main façade.
60. Detail of the large Gothic window on the first floor.
61. Detail of the arching on the upper floor.

60

61

62. Detail of the exterior railing.
63. Brick arches in the attic.
64. Detail of the brickwork of the attic arches.
65. Spatial continuity of the system of parallel arches forming the structure of the attic.

62

63

64

65

66. Vaulting of the stairwell.
67. Vaulting of the drawing room.
68. Dynamic space of the stairwell.
69. Detail of the stained glass over the main door.

66

67

68

69

Casa Calvet

In 1898 Don Pedro Mártir Calvet
commissioned the building of an apartment
block in the heart of Barcelona's
Ensanche. Building continued until 1900.
In this case, Gaudí faced for the first time
the problems of a city apartment block, a
field in which the arrangement and
exploitation of the building site had led to
extremely standardized types of
construction. Also for the first time Gaudí
began to establish his own evaluation of
the architectural possibilities permitted by
this type of urban building.

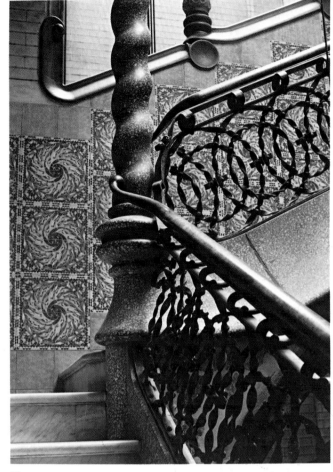

72

71

73

70. Main façade.

71. Detail of the balconies and bay windows.

72. Detail of the staircase.

73. The course of the staircase in a typical floor of the building.

74

75

76

74. Interior of the vestibule.

75. Pillar of the supporting structure of the staircase, on the ground floor.

76. The lift casing.

77. Access to the staircase and the lift.

Casa Batlló

In 1904 Don José Batlló Casanova commissioned alterations in the house on his property in the Paseo de Gracia of Barcelona. Just when the work was beginning, the house next door had been completed to the designs of the architect Puig i Cadafalch. The work of adding to and changing the building was to last until 1906, with the collaboration of several of Gaudí's assistants, amongst whom we must distinguish the components of ornamentation and colour work, contributed by Josep Maria Jujol.

78. Main façade.
79. Detail of the ornamental ceramics of the façade.
80. First floor bay window.
81. Stone structure of the bay windows on the first and second floors.

79

80

81

82

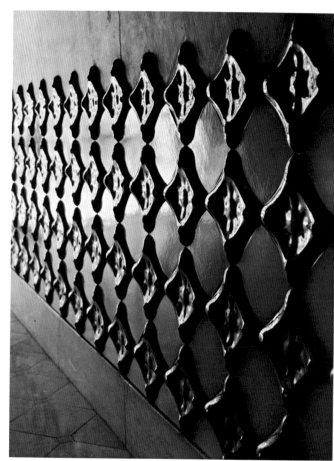

83

84

82. Vestibule and foot of the staircase.
83. Detail of the tile dado in the vestibule.
84. Graduation of colours in the tile facing of the light shaft.
85. Detail of tile facing in the light shaft.
86. Large window on the first floor.
87. Interior woodwork on the first floor.
88. Access door to apartments.

85

86

87

88

89

90

91

89. Arching in the hallway.

90. Detail of a supporting bracket in the opening of the first floor bay window.

91. Fireplace on the first floor.

92. False helicoidal ceiling on the first floor.

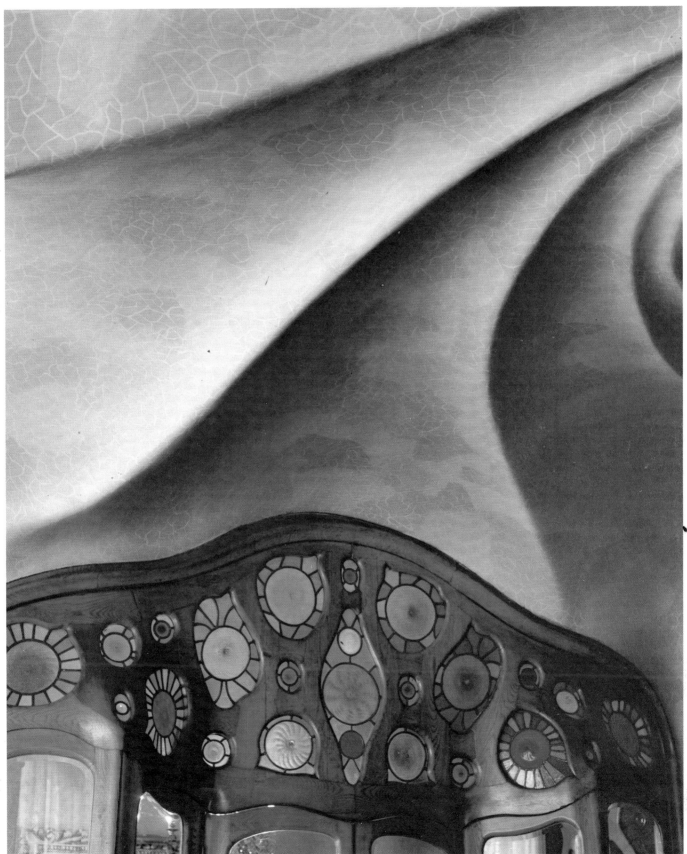

93

93. Tops of chimneys on the terrace roof.
94. The chimney finials.
95. Ceramic ornamentation of the turret and of the coping of the top of the façade.

94

Parque Güell

Eusebio Güell, Gaudi's patron and protector, was interested in promoting a residential garden area, both as a matter of speculation and as a trial of his ideas of hygiene in terms of the Garden City, of which he had become a firm advocate. Although the Parque Güell was to become a disaster from the economic point of view, the construction of its general system of services was to enable Gaudí to develop a particular idea of suburban residence and the architecture needed to serve it. The work continued from 1900 to 1914.

96-97. The name of the Parque Güell, carried out in ceramic fragments on the enclosing wall of the property.

98. Wrought iron gate.

99. Helicoidal tower, topped with Gaudí's usual double crucifix.

96

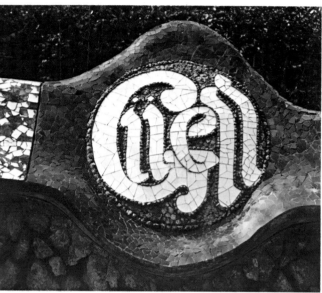

97

98

100

101

102

100-101. Flight of steps leading to the porticoed market.

102. Fountain in the form of a lizard.

103. Detail of the line of columns of the hypostyle hall of the market.

104. The hypostyle hall of the market, underneath the large plaza, with its ornamentation designed by Jujol.

103

104

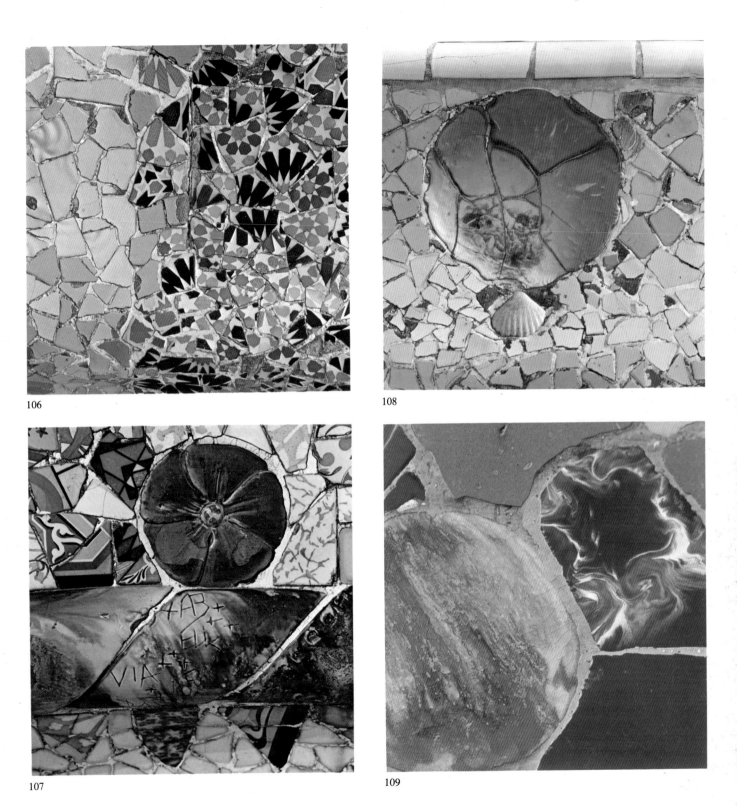

106

108

107

109

105. Course of benches faced in ceramics (carried out by Jujol)
     on top of the platform of the large plaza.

106 to 109. Details of the ornamentation carried out by Jujol
     on the bench continuing around the plaza and using the
     technique of *trencadís* (broken ceramics).

110

111

112

110. The bench on the large plaza, with the top of the porter's lodge.

111. Building for the porter's lodge, next to the main gate.

112. Wrought iron grille, originally in the Casa Vicens, now installed in the Parque Güell.

113. Detail of the roof faced with *trencadís,* on the pavilion for the porter's lodge of the Parque.

114

115

116

114. Structure of the viaduct.

115. Detail of the flower borders in the viaduct.

116. Parabolic earth-retention arches in the support walls of the viaducts.

Casa Milà (La Pedrera)

The largest apartment building which Gaudí
built in the Ensanche of Barcelona was this
complex, financed by the Milà family in the
Paseo de Gracia in 1906. Construction was to
go on until 1910, and the unusual nature of its
mass of stone in the façades led to it being
given the nickname of La Pedrera (stone
quarry).

In this building, the type of housing block with
bevelled corners which was usual in the
Ensanche of Barcelona was put completely to
one side, in order to try out a spatial and
building solution which was totally original.

117

117. Ensemble of the façades.

118. Detail of stone balconies and wrought iron grilles.

119. Detail of the capital of a support on the ground floor.

120. The relationship between materials and colours in the undulating rhythm of the façade.

119

118

120

121. Access to the first floor from the interior patio.

122. Gate of the vestibule and the carriage way.

123. Detail of a stone column in the interior patio.

124. The roughly hewn base of a column, in the access from the interior patio.

121

122

123

124

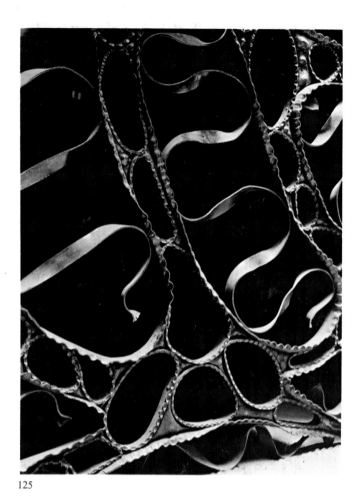

125

126

127

125 to 127. A variety of different solutions, seen in
the working of the grilles for the openings in the lower
parts of the patios.

128. View of the main patio from above.

129. The top of the façade with the terrace roof and elements
for ventilation and the chimneys.

128

129

130

130 to 134. Chimneys and ventilation openings of the apartments resolved by means of fantastic figures, which inhabit the roof terrace of the building. In the background, the Sagrada Familia under construction.

132

131

133

Alterations in the Cathedral of Palma de Mallorca

In 1904 Gaudí undertook the improvement of the Gothic building in the Catalan tradition which was most valued by Gothic specialists of the time. The project consisted of freeing the central nave from the presence of the choir and moving the choir stalls to the chancel, thus bringing about a reappraisal of all the pre-existing Gothic space, designing pulpits, canopies, lamps and choir stalls with deliriously coloured floral ornamentation.

135. The new canopy suspended over the main altar.

136. Detail of the grilles in the chancel.

137. The Archbishop's coat of arms.

138. Detail of the new wrought iron candle holders.

136

137

138

139-140. Floral ornamentation, probably the work of Jujol, in the new location of the choir in the chancel.

141. A view of the space of the central nave, seen thorough the structure of the new canopy.

139

140

Project for a hotel in New York

Although it has not been possible to prove it with complete certainty, it seems to be sure that these drawings depict the commission which Gaudí worked on in 1908 for a great skyscraper, intended for a hotel in New York.

Of this project, the only things with which we are familiar are the drawings made by the sculptor J. Matamala, in the 50s, in an attempt to recall and reconstitute what, according to this faithful disciple and assistant of Gaudí, the master's intentions had been.

142

142. Side view of the complex.

143. Front view of the complex.

144. Longitudinal section and ground plan of the building at various levels.

145. Cross section.

146. Perspective of the large interior hall.

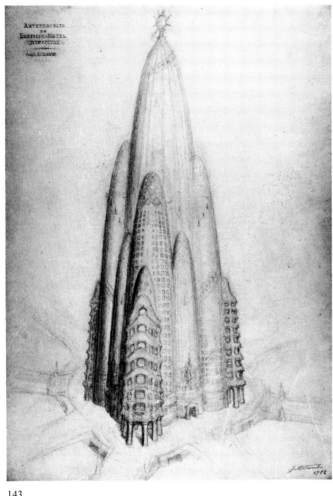

143

144

145

146

The Chapel of the Colonia Güell

The Güell family had organized one of the first industrial settlements in Spain, in order to transfer their textile industry from the outskirts of Barcelona to the village of Santa Coloma de Cervelló.

Even though Gaudí and his assistants took some part in designing the rest of the industrial colony, their most compelling work was undoubtedly the Chapel, which, dominating the site from a low mound, was meant to preside over the complex of the new township. Gaudí began to work on this plan in 1890, although the work did not begin until 1908, and it continued until at least 1915, being then for all practical purposes interrupted, with the single exception of the crypt of the future church, which was however never built.

147. View of the complex of porches in front of the crypt.

148-149. Detail of the large lateral windows of the crypt.

150. Porch and lateral façade of the crypt.

148

149

150

151

152

151. Detail of the porch at the front of the crypt.

152. Structure of irregular arcades and of inclined supports, which form the porches at the front of the entrance to the crypt.

153. Cross made from wrought iron plating.

154. System of inclined supports in the porch.

153

154

155

155. Detail of the stone columns supporting the brick arcades of the porch.
156. Interior space of the crypt.
157. Large windows in the crypt, with lantern windows.

156

Expiatory Church of the Sagrada Familia

The work was commenced by the architect Francisco de Paula del Villar in 1882, but Gaudí took over the commission in 1884, and did not cease to occupy himself with it until his death in 1926.

Conceived as a new Cathedral for the new city of Barcelona, the project underwent many modifications throughout Gaudí's lifetime.

The various stylistic stages of Gaudí's work can be recognised throughout the evolution of this task; its very condition as an unfinished fragment is a clear expression of the millenarial ideas Gaudí had of monumental architecture.

The Church, the sum total of his archictectural problems, was conceived as a synthetic experiment in the constructive, the symbolic and the monumental.

159

160

158. The façade of the Nativity.
159. Detail of a name on a capital of the façade of the Nativity.
160. Detail of the base of a column on the façade of the Nativity.
161. Interior view of the apse and eastern transept of the Church (unfinished).

162

162. Figures of angels on the façade of the Nativity.
163. Groups of animals on the façade of the Nativity.
164. Abstract geometrical finish on the interior front of the eastern transept.
165. Carving of 1882, commemorating of the beginning of the work. In the background, the towers of the façade of the Nativity.

163

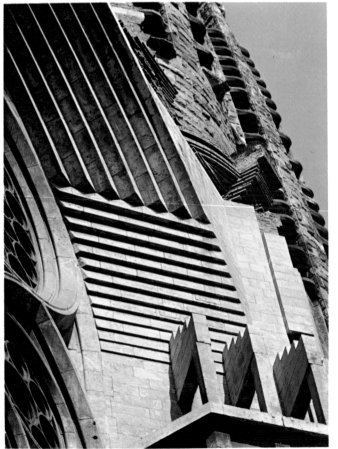

164

166. The symbol of a tree at the centre of the façade of the Nativity.

167. Relief carving of the Nativity.

168. Detail of palm trees at the base of the portal of the Nativity.

169. The triple portal of the Nativity.

166

167

168

169

170. Tops of the four towers of the façade of the Nativity.

171. The structure of the pinnacles of the apse. In the
background, the towers of the façade of the Nativity.

170

172. Abstract floral top on the apex of the portal of the Nativity.

173. Detail of the keystone of the vault of the crypt.

174. Structure of the crypt in Gothic style.

172

173

175. Model of the unfinished main and lateral naves.

LIST OF ILLUSTRATIONS